About this Learning (

G000098784

Shmoop Will Make You a Better Lover*
*of Literature, History, Poetry, Life...

Our lively learning guides are written by experts and educators who want to show your brain a good time. Shmoop writers come primarily from Ph.D. programs at top universities, including Stanford, Harvard, and UC Berkeley.

Want more Shmoop? We cover literature, poetry, bestsellers, music, US history, civics, biographies (and the list keeps growing). Drop by our website to see the latest.

www.shmoop.com

Table of Contents

Introduction 4
   In a Nutshell 4
   Why Should I Care? 4
Summary 5
   Book Summary 5
   Prologue 6
   Chapter One 7
   Chapter Two 8
   Chapter Three 9
   Chapter Four 10
   Chapter Five 10
   Chapter Six 11
   Chapter Seven 12
   Chapter Eight 13
   Chapter Nine 14
   Chapter Ten 15
   Chapter Eleven 15
   Chapter Twelve 16
   Chapter Thirteen 17
   Chapter Fourteen 17
   Chapter Fifteen 18
   Chapter Sixteen 18
   Chapter Seventeen 19
   Chapter Eighteen 19
   Chapter Nineteen 20
   Chapter Twenty 20
   Chapter Twenty-One 21
   Chapter Twenty-Two 21
   Chapter Twenty-Three 22
   Chapter Twenty-Four 22
Themes 23
   Theme of The Supernatural 23
   Questions About The Supernatural 23
   Chew on The Supernatural 23
   Theme of Innocence 23
   Questions About Innocence 23
   Chew on Innocence 24
   Theme of Good vs. Evil 24
   Questions About Good vs. Evil 24
   Chew on Good vs. Evil 24
   Theme of Appearances 24
   Questions About Appearances 25
   Chew on Appearances 25

Theme of Repression 25
Questions About Repression 25
Chew on Repression 25
Theme of Society and Class 26
Questions About Society and Class 26
Chew on Society and Class 26
Theme of Wisdom and Knowledge 26
Questions About Wisdom and Knowledge 26
Chew on Wisdom and Knowledge 27
Theme of Gender 27
Questions About Gender 27
Chew on Gender 27
Theme of Literature and Writing 27
Questions About Literature and Writing 28
Chew on Literature and Writing 28
Quotes 28
The Supernatural Quotes 28
Innocence Quotes 31
Good vs. Evil Quotes 33
Appearances Quotes 36
Repression Quotes 39
Society and Class Quotes 43
Wisdom and Knowledge Quotes 46
Gender Quotes 49
Literature and Writing Quotes 51
Plot Analysis 53
Classic Plot Analysis 53
Booker's Seven Basic Plots Analysis: Tragedy 54
Three Act Plot Analysis 55
Study Questions 55
Characters 56
All Characters 56
The Governess Character Analysis 56
The Governess Timeline and Summary 57
Miles Character Analysis 59
Miles Timeline and Summary 60
Flora Character Analysis 61
Flora Timeline and Summary 62
Peter Quint Character Analysis 62
Peter Quint Timeline and Summary 63
Miss Jessel Character Analysis 63
Miss Jessel Timeline and Summary 63
Mrs. Grose Character Analysis 64
The Uncle Character Analysis 64
Character Roles 64
Character Clues 66
Literary Devices 66

Symbols, Imagery, Allegory 66
Setting 67
Narrator Point of View 68
Genre 68
Tone 68
Writing Style 69
What's Up With the Title? 69
What's Up With the Ending? 69
Did You Know? 70
Trivia 70
Steaminess Rating 70
Allusions and Cultural References 71
Best of the Web 71
Movie or TV Productions 71
Videos 71
Images 72
Websites 72

Introduction

In a Nutshell

The Turn of the Screw is easily one of the most influential ghost stories of all time. Not only does it appeal to those of us who like a good thrill, it is also a model for any aspiring writer of suspense. Henry James's text is famous for its lasting mysterious qualities; though the story originally appeared over a hundred years ago in 1898, it still stumps readers everywhere to this day. Its many confusing twists and turns have sparked debates between critics since its publication, and the story has been examined from all kinds of different angles – from psychoanalysis to literary criticism. Part of what's so fascinating about it is the fact that James himself never clearly came out and told readers what he intended them to believe, and it's this ambiguity that makes it one of this prolific author's most famous, talked about short stories.

Why Should I Care?

Alas – if only Henry James knew what he did for the future of horror movies when he sat down to write *The Turn of the Screw*. If only he'd known that generation upon generation of "creepy child" movies would take inspiration from his influential story and inflict themselves upon viewers everywhere. Would he still have written it if he knew how many celluloid descendants it would spawn?

Think about it: the legacy of *The Turn of the Screw* can be seen in practically every horror movie that involves children – and that, friends, is a *lot* of horror movies. Many of the classics of the genre focus not on adults tormented by evil spirits, but children – think Linda Blair and her spinning head in *The Exorcist*, the horrifying/adorable anti-Christ of *The Omen*, or the ghost-whispering son in *The Shining*. And don't even get us started on the seemingly endless *Children of the Corn* series (a whole town of scary children – armed!). The list goes on and on.

When you strip away all of the extra stuff Hollywood has added on to the original freaky child concept – take away the magic powers and the propensity for violence – what you're really left with is the idea that James presents to us so horrifyingly in his original story: what's truly scary about children is their illusion of innocence, and the idea that underneath those adorable masks, they could know more than we do. James gets right at this terrifying heart of the matter, and to this day, no matter how desensitized we are to the images of white-faced children crawling out of wells and whatnot, reading *The Turn of the Screw* is still a good, old-fashioned, genuinely terrifying experience.

Summary

Book Summary

The story opens with a framing device – we find ourselves at a holiday party, where ghost stories are being told. One of the members of the party, Douglas, promises rather woefully to provide a chilling, real-life tale once a manuscript containing it arrives. The houseguests are all intrigued and excited – as are we, the readers.

Chapter One begins the proper "story." A nameless, young governess (our narrator) is hired by a dashing, rich, and rather odd man to be a governess for his niece and nephew who live at a country estate called Bly. The Governess sets out for Bly, with only the instruction that she is never to contact the uncle. At the house, she finds Mrs. Grose, a kindly housekeeper, and Flora, the younger of the children. Flora is an exceptionally beautiful and all-around wonderful child – too wonderful, perhaps.

Things are complicated when the Governess receives word that Miles, the older child, has been expelled from his school. We're not told why – but the school's headmaster sternly states that Miles will never be allowed back. The Governess wonders what the boy could possibly have done to receive such a verdict. Mrs. Grose denies that anything is wrong with Miles; when the boy himself arrives, his incredible beauty and charm convince the Governess that she was crazy to think that he could do any wrong.

Everything seems great for a little while, until the Governess sees a strange and menacing male figure on one of the castle's towers one evening. A few days later, the same stranger reappears just outside the dining room window, eerily looking in. The Governess is shocked by his return, and even more alarmed by the idea that he's not there for her – he's there for someone else. But who?...

The Governess and Mrs. Grose figure out that the mysterious figure is Peter Quint, a former servant of the children's uncle. The strangest thing is – Quint is *dead*. The Governess and the housekeeper make a pact to save the children from the ghost's evil influence.

This isn't the end of their troubles, though. Another ghost appears one day as the Governess watches over Flora. She's sure that the child also sees the ghost but pretends not to. The Governess is certain that this evil presence is that of Miss Jessel, her predecessor. What disturbs her the most is the possibility that Flora saw the ghost – but actively deceived her new teacher. Alarmingly, the next sighting is inside the house; the Governess sees Quint on a staircase, then a few days later, sees Jessel in the same place. Things are getting majorly scary.

The question of the children's innocence is still pressing. One night, the Governess discovers a weird little scene – Flora has snuck out of bed and is gazing out the window at someone on the lawn, who, in turn, is looking up at someone *else* on top of the tower. The mysterious person on the lawn is not in fact Miss Jessel, who the Governess expects, but is instead Miles. The boy

excuses himself, but the Governess is even more convinced that something fishy is going on with the children and the ghosts.

From here on out, events escalate fast – the Governess's relationship with Miles grows more and more uncomfortable and strangely intimate, while he tries to use his power over her to get her to send him away to school again. Then, Flora goes missing one day, only to be found at the lake where Miss Jessel was first sighted. Once the girl is found, the Governess loses it and demands to know where Miss Jessel is. Upon saying this, the ghost appears – but only to the Governess. Flora denies having ever seen any ghost, and poor Mrs. Grose certainly can't see the spirit. Flora turns against the Governess for good.

It's decided that Flora and Mrs. Grose will leave Bly for London, where they will go to the children's uncle (to whom the Governess has already written). Unfortunately, the Governess's letter never got sent – it turns out that Miles stole it and burned it. Furthermore, we finally learn why Miles was asked to leave school, though we don't get any details beyond the fact that he said "things" to the other boys; we're not sure what the deal is with that.

In the midst of this confession, the ghost of Peter Quint appears one last time outside the window. The Governess cries out at him, and Miles attempts to see the ghost – but he's disappeared. This seems like a triumph for the Governess...until she realizes that Miles has died in her arms.

Prologue

- Griffin finishes a very satisfactory ghost story, concerning a child who sees some terrifying apparition. The Narrator notices that Douglas has something to say.
- Two days later, Douglas brings up Griffin's story again; he wonders aloud if the terror of the story would be increased if it involved *two* children instead of one.
- Douglas cranks up the tension, telling his listeners (and readers) that the story he will tell has never been heard before – however, he can't tell it just yet.
- Apparently, the story exists only in an original manuscript, which he keeps in his office in town. It was written by a woman who was once the governess of Douglas's sister; we get the feeling that he was perhaps in love with her (or something) a long time ago. She's been dead for the past twenty years.
- The guests agree to reconvene to hear Douglas's story, once the manuscript arrives.
- The manuscript jumps right in the midst of the tale, so Douglas gives some background info: the woman in question (we'll call her the Governess), who was the daughter of a poor but good family, answers an employment ad in the newspaper, and finds herself at an interview with a handsome, wealthy, and generally rather dashing gentleman. The Governess is quite taken by her potential employer (who wouldn't be?).
- The gentleman, who lives in the city, has two young children in his care at his country home at Bly – they're his niece and nephew, who were left to him when their parents died in India. He feels bad for the kids, but doesn't exactly know what to do with them.
- The job in question sounds like a pretty good deal; she would simply have to look after the little girl, Flora, and the boy, Miles, during his school breaks. Mrs. Grose, a faithful family servant, acts as housekeeper and temporary nanny to the kids at Bly.

- Alarmingly, we hear that the previous governess died – though we don't know how.
- Douglas takes a brief break from his story to converse with the Narrator; they have a little back and forth about the Governess's motives in taking the job.
- Upon seeing her potential employer a second time, the Governess takes his offer, despite the fact that many previous applicants rejected it. The reason for this is the gentleman's rather odd final condition: he insists that once the young lady takes the job, she never contact him again, and that she should completely take over the children and all of their matters. She agrees, and feels like she's already had some kind of reward.
- After this background info, Douglas begins to read the manuscript – it's untitled, though the narrator snidely remarks that *he* has thought of a title (and it's the one we find on the cover of the book).

Chapter One

- From here on out, the Governess is our narrator. She tells us about her pleasant journey to her employer's country home, where she is met by Mrs. Grose and Flora.
- She's quite impressed with the house, and its pleasant appearance makes her admire her employer even more.
- Apparently, Flora is just the most adorable creature ever. The Governess falls for her immediately.
- Everything at Bly is quite proper so far – the Governess is installed in a gorgeous bedroom, and she feels quite pleased overall with her surroundings.
- The Governess can't sleep during her first night at Bly; she's too excited about all of the changes that have come to pass in her life. She's happy about everything, and even though she'd been a little nervous about meeting Mrs. Grose, she thinks that they'll get along just splendidly.
- The very thought of Flora quells any remaining fears the Governess has. True, she has trouble sleeping that night, and even thinks she hears some creepy sound effects (a child's cry, a footstep outside her door) – however, for the most part, she is content with her job, her student, and her new home. For now, that is…
- It's decided that, after this first night, Flora will stay in the Governess's room. That and other practical matters had been handled earlier in the evening over dinner with Flora and Mrs. Grose. The Governess recalls her discussion with the housekeeper about her other pupil, Miles.
- Miles is apparently just as darling as his little sister, and Mrs. Grose thinks that the Governess will just be "carried away" (1.6). The Governess replies that she was already carried away by the children's uncle in London…*awkward*.
- Miles is due to return from school on Friday; the Governess and Flora plan to meet him upon his arrival at Bly.
- The next day, the Governess gets acquainted with her new home. The grandeur of the house intimidates her, but she also feels proud to belong there. In an attempt to get her small pupil to like her, she asks Flora to show her around the place.
- The little girl takes her job seriously, and shows her new governess around Bly's many rooms and hallways.

- The Governess admits that, if she were to see that house again, she wouldn't be as impressed; however, on that first day, she remembers being awestruck – it looks to her like a romantic castle, rather than the "big ugly antique but convenient house" (1.9) that it is.
- The house reminds the Governess of a ship adrift, in which the inhabitants are passengers, and she, oddly enough, is the captain.

Chapter Two

- This rather surreal sense of command hits home two days later, as the Governess, with Flora in tow, goes to pick up Miles. She is unsettled by a letter she received from the children's uncle (who reminds her not to contact him with their troubles), with an enclosed letter from Miles's school.
- The letter basically says that Miles can't ever return to school, for reasons undisclosed. Though Mrs. Grose is illiterate and can't read the letter herself, the Governess interrogates Mrs. Grose about the boy; Mrs. Grose is appalled by the suggestion that Miles could be harmful to anyone. She passionately tells the Governess to withhold any judgment until she sees Miles in person.
- This eggs on the Governess's curiosity about the boy – she, in fact, can't *wait* to see him.
- Mrs. Grose suggests that Miles is as likely to be bad as Flora is; that is to say, it's impossible for him to misbehave. The Governess, won over anew by Flora's incredible cuteness, feels bad for even thinking poorly of either of the children.
- Despite her defense of Miles, the Governess notices Mrs. Grose being a little cagey as the day goes on. She confronts the poor housekeeper once more and asks if she has ever seen Miles to be bad at all.
- Mrs. Grose gets sassy and says that Miles is certainly naughty at times – after all, according to her, all boys should be a little bad sometimes.
- The Governess, attempting to delve further into this, suggests that she feels this way too, as long as the child in question doesn't corrupt others. Mrs. Grose laughs this off, asking if the Governess is afraid that Miles will corrupt *her* (creepy).
- On the day of Miles's arrival, the Governess makes one last attempt to find out more. She goes about it by asking about the former governess this time.
- There's a weird little confusion that goes on in this conversation with Mrs. Grose; the Governess suggests that the uncle in London prefers his employees to be young and pretty, while Mrs. Grose implies unintentionally that some other "he" likes everyone that way. Who, we wonder, is the "he" she's talking about? Mrs. Grose quickly claims that she's talking about the master (the children's uncle), but it's not entirely clear.
- The previous governess apparently never mentioned anything odd about Miles. This raises some suspicion in our narrator, and she inquires about how "careful" (2.23) this last governess was. Mrs. Grose replies that she was careful about some things, but not about others…we wonder what *that* means.
- The housekeeper refuses to say anything more about the previous governess. We just learn that she "went off" (2.25) before she died, but Mrs. Grose doesn't know how or why she died in the end.

Chapter Three

- This awkward conversation doesn't stop Mrs. Grose and the Governess from growing closer. Their friendship is cemented by Miles's arrival; it turns out that Mrs. Grose was right; once the Governess lays eyes on the boy, all her fears about him dissipate.
- Miles is just as adorably adorable as his sister, and he inspires an incredible feeling of tenderness in his new teacher. His physical beauty is so great that it actually exudes a sense of purity and innocence.
- The Governess, after being swept off her feet by Miles's gorgeous exterior, immediately has a talk with Mrs. Grose – all of her suspicions about the boy have been erased. She decides to do nothing about the letter of dismissal from his school, and not to write to the children's uncle.
- The two women embrace like sisters, vowing that they'll take care of the children, despite Miles's school-related troubles.
- For a while, everything is just peachy keen. The Governess and her two angelic charges enjoy the summer at Bly; though there are difficulties that lie ahead (for example, what to do with Miles's education), the women and children seem content to let everything slide a little in the summer months.
- In retrospect, the Governess sees this peaceful, idyllic time as "that hush in which something gathers or crouches" (3.8) before springing to attack. Hmm. It doesn't take a genius to see that something majorly bad is coming.
- During those summer days, the Governess enjoys taking a walk in the early evening, after the kiddies are tucked in bed and her work for the day is done. On these walks, she reflects upon the pleasure of her position in the world, and wonders if her obedience and discretion might give pleasure to her mysterious but longed for employer.
- Despite the fact that she only saw him twice, she's clearly fostering very special feelings for the children's uncle.
- One day, the Governess has an unpleasant surprise on her usually pleasant walk; as she idly daydreams of an encounter with a kind man (hopefully her employer!), she is shocked to see a man actually appear. However, he doesn't materialize on the path in front of her, as she imagines, nor is he kind at all.
- The figure the Governess sees is far off – he's standing on one of the old towers connected to the house. Even at this distance, she can see him quite clearly. He's a stranger, and the Governess suddenly feels exposed and endangered, since she is a young woman alone, confronted with an unknown man.
- The mystery man and the Governess regard each other – she can't figure out who he is and what he's doing there. He's not wearing a hat, which suggests to the Governess that he's familiar with the house and is at ease there.
- The two are too far apart to speak, but they match gazes challengingly. The man keeps staring at the Governess as he stalks around the top of the tower – creepy! We're getting goosebumps already.

Chapter Four

- The Governess's run-in from afar with the creepy stranger understandably unsettles her. She wonders if Bly might be housing some terrible secret, like an insane relative in the attic, à la *Jane Eyre*.
- She spends the rest of the evening pacing around, wondering what to do.
- When the Governess returns to the house and runs into Mrs. Grose, she decides instantly to "spare" her friend the trouble of worrying about the mystery man; she makes her excuses and runs off to her room without mentioning her bizarre encounter.
- Over the next few days, the Governess observes her surroundings, and decides that nobody in the household is playing a trick on her. She assumes that the stranger that she saw must have actually been a stranger to the house, who snuck in, checked out the house, and left.
- The Governess's fears are pushed out of her mind by the utter delight of her job. The children seem to only grow more and more wonderful day by day, and the Governess is head-over-heels in teacherly love with them.
- The only thing that mars the perfection of this job is the continuing mystery of Miles's wrongdoing at school.
- The idea that Miles could be bad grows more and more ridiculous to the Governess. He has the air of only being loved and never punished, which leads her to believe that he's never done any wrong, and never been caught doing anything. She admits to being "under the spell" (4.4) of his charm.
- One Sunday, as the Governess and Mrs. Grose prepare to go to an evening church service, the Governess goes to pick up a pair of gloves she dropped in the formal dining room. Upon entering the room, she immediately senses another presence.
- Lo and behold, just outside the window, she sees the same creepy guy she saw on the tower. She's shocked and horrified.
- The pair match gazes again, but this time, he looks away for a moment and glances around the room. This convinces the Governess that he's not there for her, he's there to find someone else.
- Inspired by this knowledge, the Governess sprints outside to confront the Peeping Tom. However, when she gets to the outside of the window, he's gone, and is nowhere to be found.
- At a loss, the Governess decides to mimic the man to try and discern what he was doing there. She looks in through the window just where he was – and, in an odd and fascinating repetition of what just happened, Mrs. Grose sees her from inside.
- Mrs. Grose's shock and horror perfectly mirrors that of the Governess when she saw the strange man outside – however, she doesn't understand what the housekeeper has to be scared of.

Chapter Five

- Mrs. Grose dashes outside to see what's wrong with the Governess – apparently, she looks just terrible. The Governess spills the beans about the strange man; she tells the

housekeeper about both encounters with him.

- Mrs. Grose questions the Governess about this man. They establish that he is certainly not a gentleman; in the words of the Governess, "He's a horror" (5.11).
- The Governess decides not to go to church, as she's afraid to leave the children alone at the house with the mystery man lurking around.
- The two women discuss the man's appearances further, wondering what his intentions were, how he got the house the first time, and what he will do in the future.
- The Governess finally gives a description of the face she saw; he's red-haired, handsome, has piercing eyes, and, as she says, he looks like an actor.
- She also claims that he's wearing someone else's nice clothes, though how she knows this, we have no idea. She reiterates her certainty that he's no gentleman.
- Mrs. Grose can't contain herself – she obviously knows this man. She affirms the fact that they're not *his* clothes, they're the master's. We get a name for the mysterious intruder, Peter Quint.
- Apparently, Quint was the master's valet when he lived at Bly. After the master left the country to return to London, Quint stayed on, and was in charge of the household. We get the feeling that this was not a good time.
- Oh yeah, and one more important fact emerges – Peter Quint is dead.

Chapter Six

- Mrs. Grose, bless her heart, immediately sides with the Governess, and doesn't question what she saw. They decide that they will do their best to shelter the children.
- It becomes clear to the Governess that Quint was there looking for Miles (again, we're not sure how she knows this…). The two women wonder what would happen if the ghost appeared to the children, and they think that this is what Quint wants.
- The Governess decides that she will try and intercept the ghost, in a manner of speaking, and therefore protect the children.
- The fact that the children never mentioned Quint seems strange to the Governess; Mrs. Grose says that Flora was too young to remember, but that Miles would know.
- Apparently Miles and Quint were close – the implication is that they were *too* close (whatever that means). Quint was apparently "too free" (5.7), not just with Miles, but with everyone.
- Quint's badness was pretty clear to everyone except the master, who had faith in his valet.
- Mrs. Grose admits that she was afraid of Quint's cleverness, and of the things he could do.
- The Governess practically accuses Mrs. Grose of not looking out for the children, to which the poor woman replies that she wasn't in charge of them – the master had placed Quint in charge of everything when he left, even the children.
- Over the following days, the women can't help but discuss their ghostly visitor. The Governess is sure that Mrs. Grose is still holding something back, but she's not sure what.
- The facts of Peter Quint's death are revealed to us – he died accidentally, as far as anyone could tell, having slipped and struck his head one night after leaving the pub.

- The Governess admits that she took a perverse kind of pleasure in working on this mystery – it makes her feel heroic and admirable. She betrays some rather egotistical feelings ["I confess I rather applaud myself as I look back!" (6.13)], and is proud of her immediate response, which is to simply protect the children. She feels even more united with her charges, since they're all endangered by the same threat.
- The Governess decides that she will set herself up as a "screen" (6.13) between the children and the horrible things around them. She begins to watch the children even more closely, in a frenzy that's almost like madness. However, soon enough she has proof that even more is going wrong than she'd realized.
- One day, Flora and the Governess are frolicking outside, having left Miles inside to finish a book. The little girl plays by the edge of a pond as her teacher looks on.
- Suddenly, the Governess senses someone else watching them – she can't see this third person, but she can feel its presence. She immediately questions this person's right to be there; though she knows that there could be any number of people walking around the estate, but she's sure it's nobody that *should* be there.
- Terrified, the Governess looks at Flora, who apparently hasn't noticed this intruder. The little girl is still absorbed in her game, and is trying to construct a little boat from two pieces of wood.
- The Governess looks up to see who their creepy visitor really is.

Chapter Seven

- After this eerie scene plays out, the Governess rushes to see Mrs. Grose. She's certain that the children know about the ghostly visitors.
- The Governess is convinced that Flora saw the strange figure by the pond and – horror of horrors – didn't say anything about it.
- Finally, we get a description of the figure by the water – this time, it was a woman, dressed in black, who is apparently just as evil and terrible as Quint. She just appeared out of nowhere across the lake, but according to the Governess, there was the awful feeling that she was actually standing really close.
- The Governess is also certain that she knows who this mystery woman is – she claims that it's the former governess, Miss Jessel.
- Mrs. Grose questions this last call, and wants to know how the Governess can be sure; after all, she never met her predecessor. However, the Governess gets all in a tizzy about how Flora knows that it's Miss Jessel, and that, if confronted, Flora would lie about it.
- A new fear dawns on the Governess – what is she *not* seeing? Are the ghosts appearing to the children when she's not around?
- Mrs. Grose, ever the optimist, tries to convince the Governess of Flora's innocence, claiming that she might not know that the ghostly Miss Jessel is bad.
- Mrs. Grose asks how the Governess knew that the woman she saw was Miss Jessel (we'd like to know, too).
- The Governess gives a rather vague description that could, in fact, be any number of women: she was wearing a rather shabby mourning dress, she was extremely beautiful, yet she was "infamous" (7.16). Also notable was the piercing gaze with which she looked

at Flora, as though she was determined to do something…no doubt something *bad*.

- This description is enough for Mrs. Grose, who finally comes out and tells the whole story of Peter Quint and Miss Jessel, who had some kind of illicit relationship. The latter was a lady, but as we already know, Quint was no gentleman. This difference in their social classes made their relationship even more scandalous.
- Again, Mrs. Grose reiterates Quint's presumptuous nature, saying menacingly that he "did what he wished" (7.20) with everyone.
- The Governess suggests that the relationship wasn't only Quint's fault, and that Miss Jessel must have wanted it, too. Mrs. Grose admits that she did, but shows some sympathy – she even says that it was a good thing that Miss Jessel escaped from Bly (and died). She claims that the relationship with Quint and its subsequent fallout was the reason that Miss Jessel left.
- Here, the Governess breaks down into tears; she fears that it's too late to save the children, and that they're lost already.

Chapter Eight

- The Governess and Mrs. Grose attempt to keep their heads on straight and not get carried away with extravagant ideas – but it's tough to stay calm when you're dealing with evil spirits.
- The two women meet that evening after everyone's asleep to rehash the mysterious sightings, and they confirm that indeed it was Quint and Miss Jessel that the Governess saw.
- The Governess herself isn't worried about any danger she might be in from the ghosts; instead, she's just worried about the possibility that they might have corrupted the children.
- Speaking of the children…immediately after seeing the ghosts, the Governess returns to her two pupils. Again, she's taken in by their beauty and innocence, and doubts her new theory – can it possibly be true that something as pure and wonderful as Flora could lie?
- The governess then goes back through the events of the day, wondering if perhaps she's just imagined Flora's complicity.
- In this review of the sighting, she sees only further proof of Flora's deception, but still doesn't want to believe it; needing to know more about the children, she pumps Mrs. Grose for more information, especially about the housekeeper's earlier assertion that Miles is naughty at times.
- The housekeeper admits that Miles has been bad once to her knowledge; before Quint died, the boy and the valet were apparently together all the time. Mrs. Grose, finding this inappropriate, approached Miss Jessel to complain. The former governess got a little snooty with her, and basically said that it was none of her business. Not to be deterred, Mrs. Grose reminded Miles that he should remember his position in life (as a young gentleman – as opposed to Quint, who was merely a servant). The response she got was not a good one.
- The horrifying thing that Miles did was basically what the Governess fears Flora did with Miss Jessel's ghost – he simply denied that he'd been hanging out with Quint.

- Mrs. Grose was appalled at his denial, and feared what Quint was doing with the boy. However, Miss Jessel approved of their relationship, and refused to do anything about it.
- The Governess wonders aloud whether or not Miles knew about the racy relationship between Miss Jessel and Peter Quint, and suspects that he knew all along and was concealing it.
- The two ladies wonder once again what Miles could have done at school to deserve being sent away forever.
- The Governess rightly guesses that, when Mrs. Grose reminded Miles that Quint was just a servant, he reminded her that she was the same – that's a way harsh thing to say, but of course she forgave him…people are always forgiving Miles for things.
- The picture of the past grows even more dismal; apparently, when Quint was with Miles, exerting his influence upon the boy, Miss Jessel was with Flora. This only confirms the Governess's worst fears that both of the children were in cahoots with their villainous elders.
- The Governess nobly (and self-consciously) tells Mrs. Grose that she's not accusing anyone of anything yet – she just has to be on the lookout from now on.

Chapter Nine

- The Governess waits it out for a few days, watching the children closely for signs of…well, of anything. Nothing particularly enlightening happens, but she's afraid that they might notice her unusually affectionate behavior.
- The children themselves are also unusually affectionate during this time, and the Governess is constantly more and more impressed and beguiled by them. They're any teacher's dream – attentive, bright, loving, and cute to boot.
- Miles is particularly exceptional. The question of where he will go to school poses itself to the governess – what will she do with him?
- The mystery of Miles's expulsion remains problematic. The Governess tries to draw the truth out, but is unsuccessful. Mostly, she spends her time playing with the kids, and tries to be with them all the time so that the ghosts have no chance to edge their way in.
- Flora and Miles are unusually peaceful siblings, and they seem to have a secret understanding – they never fight about anything. That in itself seems a little fishy to us.
- However, though everything seems to be just swell for a time, the Governess hasn't escaped the horror that lurks around Bly. Late one night, as she sits reading alone, she has a feeling that something's up. Putting her book aside, she leaves her room and creeps out into the hall.
- Walking down the lobby, she is unpleasantly surprised. Her candle mysteriously blows out and she sees that the approaching dawn made the light unnecessary, anyway.
- By the light of the window, she sees the dreadful figure of Peter Quint halfway up the stairs – this is the closest she's been to the specter. They stare each other down again; this time, oddly, she feels no fear, and stands her ground.
- The creepiest thing, to the Governess, is the total silence that passes between her and Quint…it's the only jarringly unnatural element of this meeting. They stare at each other for a painfully long moment before Quint descends the stairs and disappears.

Chapter Ten

- Shaken (but not too stirred – ha!), the Governess returns to the room she shares with Flora. There, she finds something that *does* fill her with terror – the girl is missing!
- This mystery is quickly resolved, however; Flora emerges from behind the curtains and immediately demands to know where the Governess has been. Taken aback, the Governess struggles to explain herself.
- Flora immediately explains her absence from bed, saying that she knew the Governess was gone, and that she thought someone was walking around outside. However, she denies seeing anyone.
- The Governess is convinced that Flora is lying, and for a moment is seized with the desire to confront the girl. Instead, she simply asks why Flora made her bed look as though she was still there. The little girl, unperturbed, responds that she didn't want to scare the Governess in case she returned.
- This answer is far from satisfactory to the Governess, and from this point on, she's vigilant both night and day. She even gets up in the dead of night sometimes to walk the hallways, but she never encounters Quint in the house again.
- However, the Governess does encounter another spectral visitor; she sees Miss Jessel sitting woefully on the staircase, but the woman disappears before she can confront her.
- On the eleventh night after Quint's appearance, another alarming incident happens. The Governess wakes up inexplicably in the night, and notices that that the candle she left burning has gone out – she immediately knows that Flora blew it out.
- The child has left her bed, and the Governess finds her once again at the window. The Governess is sure that Flora is in communication with the ghost of Miss Jessel, and she creeps out to find another window to see what the girl is looking at.
- Walking down the hallway, the Governess is struck with the temptation to go and confront Miles in his room – instead, she goes and eavesdrops at his door. It's totally silent.
- The Governess moves on past Miles's door, and enters another room to look out at the lawn. She sees a figure out there, looking up above her at the tower – she assumes that someone else is up there.
- The figure on the lawn, however, *isn't* Miss Jessel – it's Miles!

Chapter Eleven

- Late the next day, the Governess meets up with Mrs. Grose to reveal what she saw the previous night.
- Their meetings have been made more difficult by the Governess's constant watch over the children, but the younger woman still draws comfort from them. She speaks rather condescendingly of Mrs. Grose's complete lack of imagination, which is apparently a good thing in this context – it saves her from worrying about the children as much as she could.
- Mrs. Grose listens as the Governess relates the event of the last night. Here goes…
- The Governess went out to fetch Miles after she saw him from the window. He came to her

willingly, and she took him silently inside, back to his room. The Governess admits to feeling a little thrill of triumph at this moment; how could he possibly make up a plausible excuse for this action?

- The Governess was suddenly struck with the fear that perhaps Miles had her under his control; she felt a kind of admiration for him.
- With nothing else to do, the Governess asked Miles straight up what he was doing out on the lawn.
- He cunningly told her that he wanted to get her to think that he was a bad boy for once. He claims that he stayed up late reading, and went down to the lawn at midnight. He and Flora had planned earlier for the little girl to wake up so that the Governess would notice her at the window, and in turn notice Miles outside. He made it out to be a playful trap that the Governess walked right into.
- What are we to make of all this? We're not quite sure yet.

Chapter Twelve

- We may not be so sure what to think about the children and their mysterious nighttime escapades, but the Governess certainly knows what she thinks of all of it – she's even more convinced that the children are meeting up nightly with Quint and Jessel and that, when the children are alone together, they're talking about their ghostly friends.
- She comments rather oddly that seeing what she saw would have made Mrs. Grose crazy, but it's only served to make her (the Governess, that is) more lucid.
- The Governess comes right out and declares that the supposed innocence of the children is just a game – instead of belonging to her and Mrs. Grose, they actually belong to Peter Quint and Miss Jessel.
- Mrs. Grose, shocked and horrified, asks a good question to which we don't really receive a good answer: she asks why Quint and Jessel would do such a thing. The Governess responds confidently that it's just for the sake of evil, and that they seek to destroy the children somehow.
- The Governess comes to the conclusion that the ghosts, by appearing at a distance (like atop towers or across the lake) are trying to lure the children into pursuing them, and dying in the attempt – and the children will succumb eventually unless the two women prevent them.
- Mrs. Grose decides that only the children's uncle can possibly protect the children from this deadly harassment, and that the Governess should contact him, despite her agreement never to do so.
- The Governess disagrees strongly – after all, what could she possibly say to her employer to explain what's going on at Bly? However, Mrs. Grose remains insistent that the master should return to help with the problem.
- The Governess worries that Mrs. Grose might send for their employer.
- In a rare moment of clear self-perception, we see her worry about his scorn and contempt if she should admit to failure and call him in as backup. The Governess takes pride in her obedient service to him, and her ability to stick to the terms that he set. She's so determined to keep him out of this trouble that she threatens to leave Bly if Mrs. Grose

contacts him.

Chapter Thirteen

- Another tense month passes, and the Governess continues to keep a watchful eye on the two children. She has the odd feeling that the little group is constantly avoiding topics that hit a little too close to home.
- The Governess is getting a little paranoid – she's certain the children secretly wonder if and when she'll make some reference to Miss Jessel.
- The children are fascinated with stories of the Governess's past, and they ask to hear about her life over and over again.
- The summer is gone, and autumn falls on Bly. The ghosts don't appear again to the Governess, and she has the feeling that the house and grounds are like an empty stage after a performance.
- The lack of ghostly presence is fortunate for the Governess, but she worries about what the children might be seeing that she's not seeing. She's sure that at times the ghosts appear secretly to the children, even when she's around – her fears start to turn into obsessions.
- The Governess privately rehearses a confrontation with the children, but doesn't act on it.
- The worst fear that plagues her is the idea that the children have seen more than she has.
- However, though this eats away at her on the inside, on the outside, business is as usual. Whenever things get awkward or uncomfortable, one of the children asks promptly about their uncle. Despite the fact that he's made it clear that he won't visit or write, the children write him beautiful letters (which the Governess doesn't send).
- Adorable though the children are, the strain of constant vigilance takes its toll on the Governess. She's almost relieved when something *does* happen – though, in her comparison of the coming events to a thunderstorm, we're pretty darn sure that this "something" isn't good.

Chapter Fourteen

- Walking to church one Sunday, the Governess is struck by the idea that her command of the little family unit is like a jailer watching over prisoners, keeping an eye out for any attempt to escape.
- She recognizes, however, that, if Miles were to try and escape from her, she would have no way of stopping him – though he's just a ten-year-old boy, she recognizes his superiority of sex and class (hey, it's her idea, not ours).
- On this particular day, the prisoners revolt against their jailer. Miles asks with an innocent air when he will go back to school.
- Here is where things get a little icky. Miles and the Governess have an awkward little chat, in which we forget that he's a ten-year-old boy and she his twenty-year-old governess; instead, he seems to treat her like an equal, or even an inferior. We can't help but notice

his oddly flirtatious manner…he's a little too smooth for comfort.

- Miles suggests that it's odd for a boy to only be brought up by women, and asks if he hasn't been good enough to merit a return to school – after all, the only bad thing he's done since the Governess arrived on the scene was to go out that one night.
- The Governess pries a little further, asking whether Miles was happy at school. He replies that he's happy anywhere, but that he wants to "see more life" (14.11), which seems like a rather odd request for a ten-year-old child to make. Of course, Miles is no ordinary kid.
- Before they enter the church, Miles has one more bombshell to drop: he says that he wants to be with people of his "own sort" (14.11), though what exactly he means by that, we're not sure. The Governess suggests that he has Flora, but he scoffs at that suggestion.
- Miles wonders whether his uncle might have other ideas about what he should do, and claims that he'll convince the man to come and visit.

Chapter Fifteen

- The Governess, disturbed by this run-in with Miles, doesn't follow her party into church.
- Instead, she paces round outside, pondering what the boy just presented her with. In her eyes, Miles has figured out that she's afraid to deal with the problem of his dismissal from school, and is using her fear against her.
- For the first time since Miles showed up on the scene, the Governess wants flee from him. She returns to the house with the intention of leaving Bly for good.
- Once she gets to Bly, she's torn – but ultimately decides to go. She flies up to the schoolroom to fetch some of her things. She's not the only one there, though…a certain former governess is there already.
- The two governesses regard each other – both of them have the right to be there in that room. It's an odd moment.
- The Governess disrupts this moment of silence by calling out to Miss Jessel, calling her a "terrible miserable woman" (15.5). The ghost seems to hear her, but makes no reply. She disappears, leaving the Governess convinced that she should remain at Bly.

Chapter Sixteen

- The children and Mrs. Grose return from church, and the Governess is rather confused by the easy acceptance of her disappearance.
- The Governess tells Mrs. Grose that everything is out in the open between her and Miles.
- She goes on to say that she had a conversation with Miss Jessel (stretching the truth just a wee bit) in which the dead woman told her of the torments she suffers, into which she wants to bring Flora.
- The Governess tells Mrs. Grose that she's made up her mind to "everything" – that is, to write to her employer.
- A part of this "everything" is that the Governess resolves to tell the children's uncle about

Miles's expulsion from school. She's decided that he must have been expelled for wickedness, since he's not flawed in any other way.

- Mrs. Grose *really* doesn't want the master to get involved in Miles's potential wrongdoing; she tells the Governess that she herself will handle the situation.
- The Governess reminds her rather tactlessly that she can't write, to which she responds that she'll ask the town bailiff to write for her. However, both ladies don't want to air Bly's dirty laundry for a stranger – and so Mrs. Grose tearfully agrees to let the Governess write to the uncle.

Chapter Seventeen

- That evening, after Flora falls asleep, the Governess sits up listening to the rain and trying to write something. She can't concentrate, and goes across to listen at Miles's door.
- Being the intensely aware child that he is, Miles can tell that someone's at the door. He calls out for that someone to come in; the Governess enters rather sheepishly.
- Miles wasn't sleeping; instead, he says he was awake, thinking about their situation, and about his rather abnormal education.
- The Governess reassures the boy that he will go back to school, but that they will first find him another one. She asks about the previous school, wondering aloud why he has never talked about his previous life at all.
- The boy doesn't precisely answer the Governess's questions; he instead gets a little frustrated and tells her that his uncle must come down to settle things with her. He claims now that he doesn't want to return to the old school, but wants a new place.
- Miles refuses to tell the Governess anything more about his former life. He allows her to kiss him and try to extract more information from him, but he won't give in. He reiterates something he asked her for that morning outside church – he wants for her to leave him alone.
- The Governess tells Miles that she's begun her letter to his uncle. He asks her to finish it – but she only asks once more what happened before he returned to Bly.
- The Governess loses some of her control and swoops down upon the boy, telling him that she wants to "save" him (17.25) – this statement receives a response right away, with a sudden blast of cold air and a violent disturbance in the room.
- At this, Miles shrieks *either* in rejoicing or in fear – we're not sure which – and the Governess, shaken, looks around the room and notices that the windows are securely shut and the curtains undisturbed. Where did that cold blast come from?
- She sees that the candle's blown out somehow – and Miles says that he extinguished it.

Chapter Eighteen

- The next day, Mrs. Grose wants to confirm that the Governess has indeed written to their employer. The Governess says that she has, but neglects to mention that she hasn't sent it yet.

- The children were in particularly good form that morning in their lessons; Miles in particular seems determined to forget the events of the night before.
- Miles and the Governess play a duet on the piano, and she's distracted by his playing for some time. However, after a while, she notices that Flora is missing.
- The Governess looks around, but the little girl is nowhere to be found.
- She and Mrs. Grose both look around for the missing child, to no avail.
- The Governess is certain that Flora has gone out with Miss Jessel, while she's sure that Quint is with Miles in the schoolroom now.
- The Governess is amazed by what she sees as Miles's cleverness in eliminating her so that he and his sister could meet with their ghostly companions. The two women head outside to look for Flora and Miss Jessel.

Chapter Nineteen

- The Governess and Mrs. Grose rush to the lake, fearing what Flora might be doing there. She's even more sure than ever before that, when the children are alone, they speak of their ghostly visitors, and that they've planned this set of distractions.
- The two women find that Flora has taken the little boat that's moored at the lake. Mrs. Grose is amazed that a child could think to do all of this, but the Governess grimly states that Flora isn't always a child – sometimes she has the cunning of an old woman.
- Running around the lake, they find where Flora has ditched the boat, and they see Flora herself.
- Mrs. Grose, beside herself with relieve, seizes the child in a maternal embrace. Flora plays dumb, and simply asks where their coats and hats are. She then inquires about Miles.
- The Governess's moment of confrontation has arrived: she tells Flora that she'll let her know where Miles is *if*…(cue dramatic music) Flora will tell them where Miss Jessel is.

Chapter Twenty

- As soon as this fatal name is uttered, Flora is shocked. Mrs. Grose is also taken aback by this direct confrontation and shrieks.
- To top it all off, the Governess sees Miss Jessel herself standing across the pond.
- At this moment of terror and confusion, the Governess feels a certain triumph – now she has proof that she's not crazy! Miss Jessel's appearance exonerates her from any suspicion of madness, and proves her whole story to be true.
- However, when the Governess tries desperately to point out the apparition, Flora gives no sign of recognition – instead, she looks at the Governess with a new seriousness. Mrs. Grose loudly asserts that she doesn't see anything; the Governess feels her argument falling apart.
- Mrs. Grose, thinking fast, sides with Flora, telling her that the Governess is just joking, and that it's impossible that Miss Jessel should be there.
- Flora continues to look at the Governess coldly – and for once, she loses her aura of

perfect beauty and looks like any other petulant little girl. She lashes out against the Governess, saying that she sees nothing and has never seen anything.

- Flora ends her little tirade by begging Mrs. Grose to take her away from "*her*" – not Miss Jessel, but the Governess!
- When the Governess gets back to the house, Flora is gone, and so are her things. Miles, however, is around, and stays close to her – she has the feeling that he wants to be with her.

Chapter Twenty-One

- Early the next morning, Mrs. Grose comes to tell the Governess that Flora has fallen ill with a fever – she was kept up the night before with fears about her governess (the present one, not the former).
- The Governess is still certain that Flora's lying, and is certain that the girl will try and convince her uncle that the Governess is no good.
- The Governess decides that Mrs. Grose should take Flora away to London to see her uncle, while the Governess herself will stay at home and try to win over Miles.
- The Governess feels sure that she has to give Miles more time to come clean about the ghosts – she thinks she can still win him over to her side.
- Mrs. Grose agrees to leave with Flora, according to the Governess's plan. She agrees that this is the right thing to do – Flora, apparently, has been saying terrible things about the Governess since the day before, and Mrs. Grose fears that it's the influence of the ghosts that cause her to act this way. Despite her failure to see Miss Jessel by the pond, Mrs. Grose still believes in the Governess's story.
- One last complication presents itself: according to Mrs. Grose, the Governess's letter never made it to town. She thinks that Miles might have taken it; this act makes her imagine that his crime at school might have been the same – that of stealing letters.
- The two women part, hoping that Miles can still be "saved," and that the Governess herself can be saved and redeemed by him.

Chapter Twenty-Two

- As soon as the Governess is left alone with Miles, she misses her friend, Mrs. Grose. However, left in charge, she does her best to make everything run smoothly.
- The Governess doesn't see Miles until dinner; after the departure of his sister and Mrs. Grose, he spent the day on his own.
- The Governess struggles to act natural even in these odd circumstances. She and Miles discuss Flora's health; they eat a polite meal together while the maid is around, but, as soon as she leaves, he states, rather menacingly, that they're alone.

Chapter Twenty-Three

- Wow, is this ever awkward. The Governess and Miles, alone at last, speak cagily about Miles's explorations of the grounds over the past day or so, when he's been left to his own devices.
- Finally, it's time to get everything out in the open. The Governess insists that she's only there to help Miles and to be with him – and he sees that she wants him to tell her everything.
- As he prepares to confess, she sees for the first time that he's afraid – of her.
- Miles nervously tells the Governess that he'll tell her anything, but not just now; he says he has to go see Luke (one of the servants).
- Before she lets him go, the Governess just asks him one thing: did he take the letter she left in the hall yesterday?

Chapter Twenty-Four

- The Governess is distracted from Miles by a horrid development – she grabs the boy and holds him so that he can't see the window, for, outside, Peter Quint appears, glaring in through the windowpane.
- Miles, unaware of what's going on behind and around him, admits that he took the letter. The Governess is heartened by this admission. Miles then tells her that he found nothing in the letter, and that he burnt it.
- The Governess seizes upon this opportunity to ask about school. She asks the boy if he did, as Mrs. Grose suggested, the same kinds of thing at school.
- Miles now admits that he already knew that he could not return to school, now that he knows that the Governess knows. It's not because he stole – rather, it's because he "said things" (24.12). We never hear what kinds of things he said, but they must have been pretty bad if he was asked never to come back.
- Miles says that he only said things to those students that he liked – and that they must have in turn said these things to those that they liked.
- The Governess, however, isn't content just to speculate about these things. Instead, she presses him more, demanding to know what these things were.
- The Governess sees Quint's "white face of damnation" (24.21) once more at the window, and cries out "No more!" (24.21) to him.
- Miles, sensing that the Governess is addressing someone else, asks desperately if Miss Jessel is there – the Governess cries that it's not Miss Jessel, but another. She doesn't even refer to Quint as "he," and calls him "it" instead.
- The boy, in a fit of something like madness, asks if it's "he," meaning Quint. He then utters the most famous line of the story – "Peter Quint – you devil!" – and spins around to look for him.
- The Governess clutches at the boy, trying to tell him that Quint doesn't matter anymore, since he belongs to *her* now.
- Upon looking out the window and seeing nothing, Miles cries out – the Governess catches him and holds him, but realizes that the child, deserted by Quint's spirit, has died.

Themes

Theme of The Supernatural

What's a good ghost story without a ghost? *The Turn of the Screw* does even better than your average creepy tale – it offers readers two ghosts for the price of one. The supernatural plays a central role in this short story and, interestingly, while the ghosts we see here don't actually *do* anything, their effect is profound. James's story is horrifying not because of the supernatural elements themselves, but because of the effect they have on the minds of the living, breathing characters. Sure, the ghosts are scary…but even scarier are the things they drive the actual people to do and think.

Questions About The Supernatural

1. In your opinion, are the ghosts *really* there?
2. Does the story suggest anything about the nature of the afterlife?
3. The Governess struggles to explain why the ghosts might be haunting the children – why do you think they're sticking around? What could they hope to accomplish?

Chew on The Supernatural

The supernatural elements of *The Turn of the Screw* are simply fabrications of the Governess's mind.

The supernatural elements of *The Turn of the Screw* are undeniably real, even though the Governess is the only character to encounter them (or admit to encountering them).

Theme of Innocence

What exactly does "innocent" mean, anyway? Does it just mean free from guilt, or does it imply something a little broader – free from knowledge, perhaps? In *The Turn of the Screw*, Henry James asks his readers to ponder this question…though he never really provides an answer. However, along the way, he provides a lot of ambiguous food for thought for us to mull over; mostly they're just more questions on top of questions, which is sort of this story's general modus operandi.

Questions About Innocence

1. How innocent do you think the two children are at the end of the story? What evidence do you have either way?
2. Could Miles and Flora still be "good" kids even if they are aware of the nature of Quint and Jessel's relationship?
3. Do you think Miles deserves the punishments he receives throughout the story?

Chew on Innocence

As defined in the story, innocence can be equated with ignorance.

The only truly "innocent" character in the story is Mrs. Grose; this innocence is associated with her total lack of imagination.

Theme of Good vs. Evil

Taken at face value, *The Turn of the Screw* is about the classic struggle between good and evil: you've got your obvious bad guy, who also happens to be a creepy ghost-stalker. On the other hand, you've got your good guy, or rather, good *gal* in this case, who's defending a pair of innocent children from the grasp of the scary ghost. However, once you look below the surface, the issue gets a little more confusing. Depending on how you read the story, different characters can get assigned to the sides of good and evil...or one might decide that the black and white standards of good and evil don't even apply.

Questions About Good vs. Evil

1. Can we define the Governess as either good or evil?
2. Can we define the children as either good or evil, given the evidence we receive in the story?
3. The story does not engage with questions of religion at all – what kind of evil might Peter Quint and Miss Jessel represent?

Chew on Good vs. Evil

At its core, *The Turn of the Screw* is fundamentally a story about the struggle between good and evil.

"Good" and "evil" are eventually discarded by the end of this book; the growing ambiguity of all of the characters makes it impossible to continue to define any of them as such.

Theme of Appearances

Characters in *The Turn of the Screw* are basically judged entirely on their physical appearances – sweeping speculations are often made based simply on how people look. Hmm. Seem problematic? We know, you may be muttering, "But Shmoop, that's just so wrong!" to yourself right this very second. Don't worry, Henry James also recognizes that judging people in this fashion is not exactly the best way to go through life. The story largely revolves around questions of appearance, representation, and truth, and even if we don't emerge with any other great understanding of these things, we can be confident in saying that things aren't always as they seem.

Questions About Appearances

1. How much do the children get away with simply because of their appearance?
2. What significance might the incredible physical beauty of the children have?
3. Two other people are referred to as exceptionally beautiful – Peter Quint and Miss Jessel. What significance might this have? What makes their beauty different from the children's?

Chew on Appearances

The greatest mistake made in *The Turn of the Screw* is the equation of outer beauty with inner purity.

The dangerously spellbinding quality of the children's beauty can be considered to be one of the story's supernatural elements.

Theme of Repression

Well, seeing as *The Turn of the Screw* was published right at the tail end of the Victorian era, a period infamous for its prim, proper exterior and wild, often truly bizarre interior, you can bet that there are some very, very odd things going on underneath its surface. James shows us both the proper and decidedly improper sides of society here, and focuses on the way in which these two sides of the same coin grate against each other. The more you read repression into the story, the crazier it'll get – that's a promise! Forbidden love, falls from grace, corrupted innocents...trust us, it's all here.

Questions About Repression

1. Are we ever told what exactly happened between Miss Jessel and Peter Quint? What do we assume the nature of their relationship is?
2. The governess and Mrs. Grose are horrified to think that the children might have known about the illicit relationship between Jessel and Quint. Why is that so terrifying?
3. The specter of Miss Jessel and the Governess share two oddly intimate moments – how might this play into our understanding of the Governess's character?

Chew on Repression

The ghosts are actually a manifestation of the Governess's repressed desires, and the entire story emerges from her insanity.

The repressed desires of the Governess towards her employer play out eerily in her relationship to Miles.

Theme of Society and Class

If you take away the whole ghost thing, *The Turn of the Screw* really becomes a story about social class. Interestingly, it's still a horror story. James uses class difference to create much of the tension in the story; sure, it's scary that ghosts might be menacing a couple of adorable children, but what's even *scarier*, he tells us, is the idea the one of these ghosts might be a common, working class guy, who's endangering a rich, upper-class boy just by association.

Questions About Society and Class

1. It is noted early on that Peter Quint was not a gentleman, but Miss Jessel was a lady – how is this significant?
2. Do the Governess and Mrs. Grose's fears about Quint's influence upon Miles simply boil down to a class conflict?
3. The other adult (and the only man) in the children's lives is their guardian, the Governess's employer. Does his refusal to engage in their upbringing hint at any comment on society's treatment of children?
4. The characters are largely removed from interaction with the outside world. What does the isolation of the Bly estate contribute to our reading of the story?

Chew on Society and Class

The true danger posed by Peter Quint in *The Turn of the Screw* is not a sexual threat, but one of class, since he threatens the boundaries between servant and master.

One of the most important qualities valued in *The Turn of the Screw* is knowing one's place in the world; however, our protagonist, the Governess, consistently steps out of hers, demonstrating that she is just as much a transgressor as either Quint or Jessel.

Theme of Wisdom and Knowledge

We generally think of wisdom and knowledge as *good* things, right? In *The Turn of the Screw*, it's hard to pin knowledge down as good or bad; the best you can really do is say that knowledge is fine…for *some* people. Even though our main character is a teacher, she seems to spend most of her time hoping that her children *don't* know certain things. We get the feeling that too much knowledge too soon is dangerous, and that some people go through their whole lives poorly equipped to handle the scary truths of the world. There's even the implication that knowing too much can lead to madness – or even to death.

Questions About Wisdom and Knowledge

1. The idea that knowledge is not in fact power, but is rather corruption, is prevalent here. Why is it that Mrs. Grose, who receives all of the knowledge that the Governess has, is not also changed by the experience in any noticeable way?
2. Based on textual evidence, how much do you think the children really know?
3. How much of this story does the Governess *actually* know, and how much is simply

speculation?

Chew on Wisdom and Knowledge

The Governess's self-imposed role as a "screen" between the children and the ghosts allows her to accrue more knowledge than anyone else in the story, which in turn corrupts her to the greatest degree.

It is Miles's admission of his knowledge that ultimately kills him in the end; by dissecting the final chapter, we can see that relinquishing his secrets to the Governess also means relinquishing his life.

Theme of Gender

The world of *The Turn of the Screw* is dominated by women, whose lives in turn are dominated by men, whether they know it or not. Gender plays a huge role in the development of the rather warped network of relationships that James crafts here; though sexuality is never, *ever* openly discussed, you can be sure that James meant for his readers to ponder the various permutations of desire and power that arise out of gender struggles. Part of the difficulty is the question of how much a woman can truly control a man – or even a male child. Even in our more equitable era, it's easy to see the issues that James gets at here.

Questions About Gender

1. Miles is the only truly vocal male character – what is the significance of this?
2. What might Miles have meant by his passionate statement that he wants to be with people "of his own sort?"
3. How do Flora's and Miles's genders play out in the Governess's individual relationships to them?
4. Is Miles forgiven for more simply because he is a boy?

Chew on Gender

James emphasizes the simultaneously ridiculous and eerie precocity of Miles's character to depict him as a man in a house full of women.

The idea of Miles's possession by the spirits is more menacing than Flora's because he is male, and therefore ultimately more capable of harm.

Theme of Literature and Writing

Yes, *The Turn of the Screw* is simply a great story for the sake of being a story – but it's also a great comment upon the art of writing or telling a tale. James sets up his piece within an interesting framework that raises our awareness of its story-ness from the very first page; instead of just jumping right in with the main body of text, he starts out with a brief, seemingly

unimportant prologue. The latter does some practical things, like giving us some background info on our main character, but mostly, it just functions to create a ton of tension without a single thing happening. In this brief section, James demonstrates for us what a good horror story does – leave us breathless and excited, waiting for whatever will happen next.

Questions About Literature and Writing

1. How do you respond to the narrative frame (the first section) – why doesn't James just jump right into the governess's tale?
2. We essentially have three narrators – the actual narrator present in the untitled introductory section, Douglas (who reads the story aloud), and the Governess. What function does this triple-layered narration perform, if any?
3. Do you think James intends for this story to be a horror story in the conventional sense? What other intentions might he have had for it?

Chew on Literature and Writing

The extensive build-up before the story even begins takes readers through a skillful writerly game; James playfully works his readers into a fury of curiosity to demonstrate the power of the writer in consciously creating suspense.

While "The Turn of the Screw" is certainly a horror story of the highest caliber, it is also a kind of manual for writers of horror fiction – the title's reference to building a story suggests that it is not the *plot* that matters, but the conscious crafting of the tale

The Supernatural Quotes

"I quite agree – in regard to Griffin's ghost, or whatever it was – that its appearing first to the little boy, at so tender an age, adds a particular touch. But it's not the first occurrence of its charming kind that I know to have involved a child. If the child gives the effect another turn of the screw, what do you say to two children – ?"

"We say, of course," somebody exclaimed, "that they give two turns! Also that we want to hear about them." (Prologue.2)

Thought: The association of children with the supernatural and the heightened tension that this relationship creates is introduced early on – actually, on the very first page of the story – giving readers an idea of what to anticipate.

But it was a comfort that there could be no uneasiness in a connection with anything so beatific as the radiant image of my little girl, the vision of whose angelic beauty had probably more than anything else to do with me restlessness that, before morning, made me several times rise and wander about my room to take in the whole picture and prospect; to watch, from my open window, the faint summer dawn, to look at such portions of the rest of the house as I could catch, and to listen, while, in the fading dusk, the first birds began to twitter, for the possible recurrence of a sound or two, less natural and not without, but within, that I had fancied I heard. There had been a moment when I believed I recognized, faint and far, the cry of a child; there had been another when I found myself just consciously starting as at the passage, before my door, of a light footstep. But these fancies were not marked enough not to be thrown off, and it is only in the light, or the gloom, I should rather say, of other and subsequent matters that they now come back to me. (1.3)

Thought: Here, the whole "ghost story" genre makes itself clear; the sounds the Governess hears in the night are universally stereotypical sound effects of horror.

It was as if, while I took in – what I did take in – all the rest of the scene had been stricken with death. I can hear again, as I write, the intense hush in which the sounds of evening dropped. The rooks stopped cawing in the golden sky, and the friendly hour lost, for the minute, all its voice. But there was no other change in nature, unless indeed it were a change that I saw with a stranger sharpness. The gold was still in the sky, the clearness in the air, and the man who looked at me over the battlements was as definite as a picture in a frame. That's how I thought, with extraordinary quickness, of each person that he might have been and that he was not. We were confronted across our distance quite long enough for me to ask myself with intensity who then he was and to feel, as an effect of my inability to say, a wonder that in a few instants more became intense. (3.11)

Thought: The unnatural quality of Quint's appearance, even before we know he's a ghost, is notable straight away. The sudden dropping away of the natural world draws attention to the wrongness of his presence.

She hung fire so long that I was still more mystified. "He went, too," she brought out at last.

"Went where?"

Her expression, at this, became extraordinary. "God knows where! He died."

"Died?" I almost shrieked.

She seemed fairly to square herself, plant herself more firmly to utter the wonder of it. "Yes. Mr. Quint is dead." (5.27-29)

Thought: All of James's characters are skillful masters of suspense, whether they know it or not, even good old Mrs. Grose. This scene could easily have played out in a much less dramatic way, but James goes all out, and plays up the scare factor to the max.

[…] the thing was as human and hideous as a real interview: hideous just because it was human, as human as to have met alone, in the small hours, in a sleeping house, some enemy, some adventurer, some criminal. It was the dead silence of our long gaze at such close quarters that gave the whole horror, huge as it was, its only note of the unnatural. If I had met a murderer in such a place and at such an hour, we still at least would have spoken. Something would have passed, in life, between us; if nothing had passed, one of us would have moved. The moment was so prolonged that it would have taken but little more to make me doubt if even I were in life. (9.6)

Thought: Again, the same eerie total silence we noticed before with Quint's appearance takes over, emphasizing his almost-but-not-quite-human presence. The supernatural is always signaled by some kind of announcement here, whether it's just a feeling on the part of the Governess, or a notable change in atmosphere.

the question of her naming him has already been raised here

"Dear little Miles, dear little Miles, if you knew how I want to help you! It's only that, it's nothing but that, and I'd rather die than give you a pain or do you a wrong – I'd rather die than hurt a hair of you. Dear little Miles" – oh, I brought it out now even if I should go too far – "I just want you to help me to save you!" But I knew in a moment after this that I had gone too far. The answer to my appeal was instantaneous, but it came in the form of an extraordinary blast and chill, a gust of frozen air, and a shake of the room as great as if, in the wild wind, the casement had crashed in. The boy gave a loud, high shriek, which, lost in the rest of the shock of sound, might have seemed, indistinctly, though I was so close to him, a note either of jubilation or of terror. I jumped to my feet again and was conscious of darkness. So for a moment we remained, while I stared about me and saw the drawn curtains were unstirred and the window tight. "Why, the candle's out!" I then cried.

"It was I who blew it, dear!" said Miles. (17.25)

Thought: The supernatural forces that have swirled around the story up until this point actually let loose here for the first time – the burst of cold air and the mysterious wind are the first actual manifestations of ghostly power that we see.

But he had already jerked straight round, stared, glared again, and seen but the quiet day. With the stroke of the loss I was so proud of he uttered the cry of a creature hurled over an abyss, and the grasp with which I recovered him might have been that of catching him in his fall. I caught him, yes, I held him – it may be imagined with what a passion; but at the end of a minute I began to feel what it truly was that I held. We were alone with the quiet day, and his little heart, dispossessed, had stopped. (24.26) *miles was a ghost?*

Thought: Huh. What, we ask, really caused Miles's death? Was it simply the shock of the bizarre events that unfold around him, or was it actually true that Quint was somehow possessing his soul – and when the ghost disappears, he took Miles's life with him?

or, miles was a ghost all along, and the first time she let herself go enough to hold him, she felt his lack of nearness.

Innocence Quotes

I held [Mrs. Grose] tighter. "You like them with the spirit to be naughty?" Then, keeping pace with her answer, "So do I!" I eagerly brought out. "But not to the degree to contaminate – "

"To contaminate?" – my big word left her at a loss. I explained it. "To corrupt."

She stared, taking my meaning in; but it produced in her an odd laugh. "Are you afraid he'll corrupt you?" (2.16-18)

Thought: There's a fine line to walk between just plain naughty and actually *bad* – we're not sure which side of the line little Miles falls on.

I was a little late on the scene, and I felt, as he stood wistfully looking out for me before the door of the inn at which the coach had put him down, that I had seen him, on the instant, without and within, in the great glow of freshness, the same positive fragrance of purity, in which I had, from the first moment, seen his little sister. He was incredibly beautiful, and Mrs. Grose had put her finger on it: everything but a sort of passion of tenderness for him was swept away by his presence. What I then and there took him to my heart for was something divine that I have never found to the same degree in any child – his indescribable little air of knowing nothing in the world but love. It would have been impossible to carry a bad name with a greater sweetness of innocence, and by the time I had got back to Bly with him I remained merely bewildered – so far, that is, as I was not outraged – by the sense of the horrible letter locked up in my room, in a drawer. (3.1)

Thought: Miles's innocence apparently announces itself in his physical presence; there's something almost magical about the way in which his appearance convinces the Governess that he's a good kid.

[Miles] made the whole charge absurd. My conclusion bloomed there with the real rose-flush of his innocence: he was only too fine and fair for the little horrid unclean school-world, and he had paid a price for it. (4.3)

Thought: Miles's angelic appearance wins over the Governess right away – so much so that she is swayed into thinking that the school must have been wrong in sending him away. There's something eerie about how fully she's entranced by Miles's beauty and his aura of purity; it's almost as though he has brainwashed her into thinking that he's better than the rest of the world.

Both the children had a gentleness – it was their only fault, and it never made Miles a muff – that kept them (how shall I express it?) almost impersonal and certainly quite unpunishable. They were like those cherubs of the anecdote who had – morally at any rate – nothing to whack! (4.4)

Thought: This rather bizarre-sounding quote serves to emphasize just how oddly (creepily, one might even say) innocent and angelic these children are. The whole thing about the cherubs with nothing to whack refers to a famous story related by author Charles Lamb, who lamented the fact that a former teacher, who was fond of corporal punishment, would have no students' bottoms to whip in heaven, since angels were frequently pictured as winged baby heads with no bodies. Weird, we know.

He had never for a second suffered. I took this as a direct disproof of his having really been chastised. If he had been wicked he would have "caught" it, and I should have caught it by the rebound – I should have found the trace. I found nothing at all, and he was therefore an angel. (4.4)

Thought: The Governess's faith in Miles's innocence again seems to rest simply on his outward aspect; we actually have no idea what he's like on the inside. The Governess's certainty that she'd be able to tell if he'd ever been bad is truly, truly naïve.

Then I saw something more. The moon made the night extraordinarily penetrable and showed me on the lawn a person, diminished by distance, who stood there motionless and as if fascinated, looking up to where I had appeared – looking, that is, not so much straight at me as at something that was apparently above me. There was clearly another person above me – there was a person on the tower; but the presence on the lawn was not in the least what I had conceived and had confidently hurried to meet. The presence on the lawn – I felt sick as I made it out – was poor little Miles himself. (10.8)

Thought: Despite the fact that Miles is clearly being "bad" here, he's still depicted as "poor little Miles," as though his air of innocence still protects him somehow.

Not a sound, on the way, had passed between us, and I had wondered – oh, how I had wondered! – if he were groping about in his little mind for something plausible and not too grotesque. It would tax his invention, certainly, and I felt, this time, over his real embarrassment, a curious thrill of triumph. It was a sharp trap for the inscrutable! He couldn't play any longer at innocence; so how the deuce would he get out of it? (11.3)

Thought: Here, the Governess begins to wonder if the whole innocent and pure aura that surrounds Miles is just an act; her perceptions not only of the children but of the world around her begin to change from here on out.

What it was most impossible to get rid of was the cruel idea that, whatever I had seen, Miles and Flora saw more – things terrible and unguessable and that sprang from dreadful passages of intercourse in the past. (13.4)

Thought: The Governess's fear that the children have been corrupted by their communication with the ghosts makes us wonder what *her* state of innocence is – having seen some of what they've seen, has she also been corrupted somehow?

Those he liked? I seemed to float not into clearness, but into a darker obscure, and within a minute there had come to me out of my very pity the appalling alarm of his being perhaps innocent. It was for the instant confounding and bottomless, for if he were innocent, what then on earth was I? Paralyzed, while it lasted, by the mere brush of the question, I let him go a little, so that, with a deep-drawn sigh, he turned away from me again; which, as he faced toward the clear window, I suffered, feeling that I had nothing now there to keep him from. (24.16)

Thought: The confusion surrounding what exactly Miles did at school (it's often thought that his mysterious offense and the things he said might have been homosexual in nature) makes the Governess throw into question who is guilty and who is innocent – can it be that she's the corrupt one for putting a child into such a miserable position?

Good vs. Evil Quotes

I got hold of this; then, instinctively, instead of returning as I had come, went to the window. It was confusedly present to me that I ought to place myself where he had stood. I did so; I applied my face to the pane and looked, as he had looked, into the room. As if, at this moment, to show me exactly what his range had been, Mrs. Grose, as I had done for himself just before, came in from the hall. With this I had the full image of a repetition of what had already occurred. She saw me as I had seen my own visitant; she pulled up short as I had done; I gave her something of the shock that I had received. She turned white, and this made me ask myself if I had blanched as much. She stared, in short, and retreated on just my lines, and I knew she had then passed out and come round to me and that I should presently meet her. I remained where I was, and while I waited I thought of more things than one. But there's only one I take space to mention. I wondered why she should be scared. (4.6)

Thought: This role reversal is really fascinating – the replacement of Quint with the Governess is the first thing that makes us wonder what her deal really is. The line "I wondered why *she* should be scared" implies that perhaps the Governess has horrifying qualities of her own that she's not yet aware of.

"Another person – this time; but a figure of quite as unmistakable horror and evil: a woman in black, pale and dreadful – with such an air also, and such a face! – on the other side of the lake. I was there with the child – quiet for the hour; and in the midst of it she came." (7.3)

Thought: Miss Jessel apparently just exudes "evil" – we're not sure how or why the Governess feels this way, though. This is just part of our narrator's desire to pin things down as either good or evil, even when they don't comfortably fit in these categories.

The apparition had reached the landing halfway up and was therefore on the spot nearest the window, where at sight of me, it stopped short and fixed me exactly as it had fixed me from the tower and from the garden. He knew me as well as I knew him; and so, in the cold, faint twilight, with a glimmer in the high glass and another on the polish of the oak stair below, we faced each other in our common intensity. He was absolutely, on this occasion, a living, detestable, dangerous presence. But that was not the wonder of wonders; I reserve this distinction for quite another circumstance: the circumstance that dread had unmistakably quitted me and that there was nothing in me there that didn't meet and measure him. (9.5)

Thought: In this struggle between good and evil (or at least, between two parties vaguely representing the latter), the Governess and Quint are equally matched – and this equality adds to the rather ambiguous nature of the Governess's character.

I drew a great security in this particular from her mere smooth aspect. There was nothing in her fresh face to pass on to others my horrible confidences. She believed me, I was sure, absolutely: if she hadn't I don't know what would have become of me, for I couldn't have borne the business alone. But she was a magnificent monument to the blessing of a want of imagination, and if she could see in our little charges nothing but their beauty and amiability, their happiness and cleverness, she had no direct communication with the sources of my trouble. If they had been at all visibly blighted or battered, she would doubtless have grown, on tracing it back, haggard enough to match them; as matters stood, however, I could feel her, when she surveyed them, with her large white arms folded and the habit of serenity in all her look, thank the Lord's mercy that if they were ruined the pieces would still serve. (11.1)

Thought: The only character that is undoubtedly "good" in this story is Mrs. Grose – we never once question her innate goodness or loyalty, though all the other characters are potentially either good or evil – or both.

"They're not mine – they're not ours. They're his and they're hers!"

"Quint's and that woman's?"

"Quint's and that woman's. They want to get to them."

Oh, how, at this, poor Mrs. Grose appeared to study them! "But for what?"

"For the love of all the evil that, in those dreadful days, the pair put into them. And to ply them with that evil still, to keep up the work of demons, is what brings the others back." (12.2-3)

Thought: Interestingly, though the idea of evil is omnipresent in the story, it's never given an explanation – as far as we know, Quint and Jessel are really just evil for evil's sake.

Tormented, in the hall, with difficulties and obstacles, I remember sinking down at the foot of the staircase – suddenly collapsing there on the lowest step and then, with a revulsion, recalling that it was exactly where more than a month before, in the darkness of night and just so bowed with evil things I had seen the specter of the most horrible of women. (15.4)

Thought: Again, the Governess's alignment with the ghosts – this time with Miss Jessel – makes us question whether she herself is good or evil, or if anyone can concretely be defined in such a manner.

"I've made up my mind. I came home, my dear," I went on, "for a talk with Miss Jessel."

I had by this time formed the habit of having Mrs. Grose literally well in hand in advance of my sounding that note: so that even now, as she bravely blinked under the signal of my word, I could keep her comparatively firm. "A talk! Do you mean she spoke?"

"It came to that. I found her, on my return, in the schoolroom."

"And what did she say?" I can hear the good woman still, and the candor of her stupefaction.

"That she suffers the torments – !"

It was this, of a truth, that made her, as she filled out my picture, gape. "Do you mean," she faltered," – of the lost?"

"Of the lost. Of the damned." (16.6-7)

Thought: Hmm...*interesting*. Who's being deceptive now, Governess? We don't know why the Governess decides to fabricate this little section of the story – after all, we saw her interaction with Miss Jessel in the schoolroom, and there was no conversation that we could see. However, here she tells Mrs. Grose that she's received confirmation that the ghost is damned. Can it be that the Governess is just trying to create her own justification for her actions by bringing religion into it?

The appearance was full upon us that I had already had to deal with here: Peter Quint had come into view like a sentinel before a prison. The next thing I saw was that, from outside, he had reached the window, and then I knew that, close to the glass and glaring in through it, he offered once more to the room his white face of damnation. It represents but grossly what took place within me at the sight to say that on the second my decision was made; yet I believe that no woman so overwhelmed ever in so short a time recovered her grasp of the act. It came to me in the very horror of the immediate presence that the act would be, seeing and facing what I saw and faced, to keep the boy himself unaware. The inspiration – I can call it by no other name

– was that I felt how voluntarily, how transcendently, I might. It was like fighting with a demon for a human soul, and when I had fairly so appraised it I saw how the human soul – held out, in the tremor of my hands, at arm's length – had a perfect dew of sweat on a lovely childish forehead. (24.1)

Thought: The struggle between good and evil is made perfectly clear here – Quint and the Governess are actually fighting over Miles's soul.

[…] he was at me in a white rage, bewildered, glaring vainly over the place and missing wholly, though it now, to my sense, filled the room like the taste of poison, the wide, overwhelming presence. "It's he?"

I was so determined to have all my proof that I flashed into ice to challenge him. "Whom do you mean by 'he'?"

"Peter Quint – you devil!" His face gave again, round the room, its convulsed supplication. " Where?"

They are in my ears still, his supreme surrender of the name and his tribute to my devotion. "What does he matter now, my own? – what will he ever matter? I have you," I launched at the beast, "but he has lost you forever!" Then, for the demonstration of my work, "There, there!" I said to Miles. (24.22-25)

Thought: In the Governess's triumphant eyes, Quint has lost the battle for Miles – however, the boy's wording makes it unclear who is the "devil" here, the Governess or Quint.

Appearances Quotes

But it was a comfort that there could be no uneasiness in a connection with anything so beatific as the radiant image of my little girl, the vision of whose angelic beauty had probably more than anything else to do with me restlessness that, before morning, made me several times rise and wander about my room to take in the whole picture and prospect. (1.3)

Thought: From the very first day, the children's physical beauty is a distraction; here, Flora's "radiant image" is so wonderful that it keeps the Governess up all night thinking about her new life with the child.

"And the little boy – does he look like her? Is he too so very remarkable?"

One wouldn't flatter a child. "Oh, miss, most remarkable. If you think well of this one!" – and she stood there with a plate in her hand, beaming at our companion, who looked from one of us to the other with placid heavenly eyes that contained nothing to check us.

"Yes; if I do – ?"

"You will be carried away by the little gentleman!" (1.4-6)

Thought: The children's appearance does have the effect of "carrying away" viewers – though it seems benign at this point, we begin to wonder about the spell the cast on the women as the story goes on.

I have not seen Bly since the day I left it, and I daresay that to my older and more informed eyes it would now appear sufficiently contracted. But as my little conductress, with her hair of gold and her frock of blue, danced before me round corners and pattered down passages, I had the view of a castle of romance inhabited by a rosy sprite, such a place as would somehow, for diversion of the young idea, take all color out of storybooks and fairytales. Wasn't it just a storybook over which I had fallen adoze and adream? No; it was a big, ugly, antique, but convenient house, embodying a few features of a building still older, half-replaced and half-utilized, in which I had the fancy of our being almost as lost as a handful of passengers in a great drifting ship. Well, I was, strangely, at the helm! (1.9)

Thought: The whole house falls under the glamour of Flora's charm, and the Governess's view of her whole situation is colored by her infatuation with the child.

"See him, miss, first. Then believe it!" I felt forthwith a new impatience to see him; it was the beginning of a curiosity that, for all the next hours, was to deepen almost to pain. Mrs. Grose was aware, I could judge, of what she had produced in me, and she followed it up with assurance. "You might as well believe it of the little lady. Bless her," she added the next moment – "look at her!" (2.10)

Thought: The idea that Miles's innocence could be proven by simply looking at him is more than a little odd – Mrs. Grose's faith in her charges seems to be founded purely on their adorability, which, as far as we know, doesn't usually correlate directly to morality.

As soon as I could compass a private word with Mrs. Grose I declared to her that it was grotesque.

She promptly understood me. "You mean the cruel charge – ?"

"It doesn't live an instant. My dear woman, look at him!"

She smiled at my pretension to have discovered his charm. "I assure you, miss, I do nothing else! What will you say, then?" she immediately added.

"In answer to the letter?" I had made up my mind. "Nothing."

"And to his uncle?"

I was incisive. "Nothing."

"And to the boy himself?"

I was wonderful. "Nothing." (3.1-5)

Thought: This wording is really interesting…the women have only to look at Miles to know that he's innocent, but that's not all – Mrs. Grose's response ("I do nothing else!") hints at the oddly obsessive pleasure of looking at the kid.

My charming work was just my life with Miles and Flora, and through nothing could I so like it as through feeling that I could throw myself into it in trouble. The attraction of my small charges was a constant joy, leading me to wonder afresh at the vanity of my original fears, the distaste I had begun by entertaining for the probable gray prose of my office. There was to be no gray prose, it appeared, and no long grind; so how could work not be charming that presented itself as daily beauty? It was all the romance of the nursery and the poetry of the school room. I don't mean by this, of course, that we studied only fiction and verse; I mean I can express no otherwise the sort of interest my companions inspired. (4.3)

Thought: The Governess's infatuation with her young pupils influences everything about her new job; the whole thing takes on the appearance of flawless romance.

Of course I was under the spell, and the wonderful part is that, even at the time, I perfectly knew I was. But I gave myself up to it; it was an antidote to any pain, and I had more pains than one. I was in receipt in these days of disturbing letters from home, where things were not going well. But with my children, what things in the world mattered? That was the question I used to put to my scrappy retirements. I was dazzled by their loveliness. (4.4)

Thought: Again, we see the magical nature of the children's beauty…they actually take away the Governess's other cares. After all, how often do you seriously find yourself "dazzled" by anyone's loveliness?

He was the same – he was the same, and seen, this time, as he had been seen before, from the waist up, the window, though the dining room was on the ground floor, not going down to the terrace on which he stood. His face was close to the glass, yet the effect of this better view was, strangely, only to show me how intense the former had been. He remained but a few seconds – along enough to convince me he also saw and recognized; but it was as if I had been looking at him for years and had known him always. Something, however, happened this tune that had not happened before; his stare into my face, through the glass and across the room, was as deep and hard as then, but it quitted me for a moment during which I could still watch it, see it fix successively several other things. On the spot there came to me the added shock of a certitude that it was not for me he had come there. He had come for someone else. (4.5)

Thought: Like with everyone else, the Governess makes a snap judgment on Peter Quint – she has total faith in her perception of his appearance.

"Why, of the very things that have delighted, fascinated, and yet, at bottom, as I now so strangely see, mystified and troubled me. Their more than earthly beauty, their absolutely unnatural goodness. It's a game," I went on; "it's a policy and a fraud!"

"On the part of little darlings – ?"

"As yet mere lovely babies? Yes, mad as that seems!" The very act of bringing it out really helped me to trace it – follow it all up and piece it all together. "They haven't been good – they've only been absent. It has been easy to live with them, because they're simply leading a life of their own. They're not mine – they're not ours. They're his and they're hers!" (12.2)

Thought: For the first time, the Governess actually questions the policy of just taking people at face value and questions the system of believing everything one sees that dominates the first half of the book. However, if you're used to living in a world in which first impressions mean everything, as the Governess is, it's a big, traumatic shock to realize that things aren't always what they seem.

Flora continued to fix me with her small mask of reprobation, and even at that minute I prayed God to forgive me for seeming to see that, as she stood there holding tight to our friend's dress, her incomparable childish beauty had suddenly failed, had quite vanished. I've said it already – she was literally, she was hideously, hard; she had turned common and almost ugly. "I don't know what you mean. I see nobody. I see nothing. I never have. I think you're cruel. I don't like you!" Then, after this deliverance, which might have been that of a vulgarly pert little girl in the street, she hugged Mrs. Grose more closely and buried in her skirts the dreadful little face. In this position she produced an almost furious wail. "Take me away, take me away – oh, take me away from her!"

"From me?" I panted.

"From you – from you!" she cried. (20.5)

Thought: In the Governess's eyes, this confirmation of Flora's deceitfulness takes away her physical beauty – here, we see the link between innocence and beauty clearly laid out.

Repression Quotes

"[…] It sounded dull – it sounded strange; and all the more so because of his main condition."

"Which was – ?"

"That she should never trouble him – but never, never: neither appeal nor complain nor write

about anything; only meet all questions herself, receive all moneys from his solicitor, take the whole thing over and let him alone. She promised to do this, and she mentioned to me that when, for a moment, disburdened, delighted, he held her hand, thanking her for the sacrifice, she already felt rewarded.

"But was that all her reward?" one of the ladies asked.

"She never saw him again." (Prologue.18)

Thought: As a proper young lady, we can imagine that the Governess doesn't often feel the touch of a man – and so this brief contact with her dashing employer seems like enough of a reward for the isolated life she's about to embark upon.

It was a pleasure at these moments to feel myself tranquil and justified; doubtless, perhaps, also to reflect that by my discretion, my quiet good sense and general high propriety, I was giving pleasure – if he ever thought of it! – to the person to whose pressure I had responded. What I was doing was what he had earnestly hoped and directly asked of me, and that I could, after all, do it proved even a greater joy than I had expected. I daresay I fancied myself, in short, a remarkable young woman and took comfort in the faith that this would more publicly appear. (3.9)

Thought: While the Governess never comes right out and admits that she's carrying a blazing torch for the children's uncle, she indulges in a lot of speculation about him and the, er, "pleasure" she might bring him.

One of the thoughts that, as I don't in the least shrink now from noting, used to be with me in these wanderings was that it would be as charming as a charming story suddenly to meet someone. Someone would appear there at the turn of a path and would stand before me and smile and approve. I didn't ask more than that – I only asked that he should know and the only way to be sure he knew would be to see it, and the kind light of it, in his handsome face. (3.10)

Thought: Ah, so what the Governess is *really* seeking is male approval – her wildest fantasy, it appears, is that of finding someone to validate her.

I quickly rose, and I think I must have shown her a queerer face than ever yet. "You see me asking him for a visit?" No, with her eyes on my face she evidently couldn't. Instead of it even –as a woman reads another – she could see what I myself saw: his derision, his amusement, his contempt for the breakdown of my resignation at being left alone and for the fine machinery I had set in motion to attract his attention to my slighted charms. She didn't know – no one knew – how proud I had been to serve him and to stick to our terms; yet she nonetheless took the measure, I think, of the warning I now gave her. "If you should so lose your head as to appeal to him for me – "

She was really frightened. "Yes, miss?"

"I would leave, on the spot, both him and you." (12.9-10)

Thought: The Governess still can't come to terms with her desire for her employer, which she continues to displace into her feelings about her job – her dire need to follow the rules he set is her only means of expressing her love for him.

Transcribed here the speech sounds harmless enough, particularly as uttered in the sweet, high, casual pipe with which, at all interlocutors, but above all at his eternal governess, he threw off intonations as if he were tossing roses. There was something in them that always made one "catch," and I caught, at any rate, now so effectually that I stopped as short as if one of the trees of the park had fallen across the road. There was something new, on the spot, between us, and he was perfectly aware that I recognized it, though, to enable me to do so, he had no need to look a whit less candid and charming than usual. I could feel in him how he already, from my at first finding nothing to reply, perceived the advantage he had gained. (14.2)

Thought: The Governess can't – or *won't* – put her finger on what has changed between her and Miles. We can only note that he grows more and more like a man and less childish as the story goes on, and his greater degree of independence also gives him a greater sense of power – in our eyes and in those of his teacher.

Dishonored and tragic, she was all before me; but even as I fixed and, for memory, secured it, the awful image passed away. Dark as midnight in her black dress, her haggard beauty and her unutterable woe, she had looked at me long enough to appear to say that her right to sit at my table was as good as mine to sit at hers. While these instants lasted, indeed, I had the extraordinary chill of feeling that it was I who was the intruder. It was as a wild protest against it that, actually addressing her – "You terrible, miserable woman!" – I heard myself break into a sound that, by the open door, rang through the long passage and the empty house. (15.5)

Thought: Miss Jessel is depicted with some amount of sympathy here and throughout the story; though she is certainly described as an evil presence, the Governess is also clearly fascinated with her. We wonder if Miss Jessel is a kind of evil twin to the Governess – the shamed woman acts upon her desires and suffers the consequences, while the Governess keeps hers bottled up inside.

It made me, the sound of the words, in which it seemed to me that I caught for the very first time a small faint quaver of consenting consciousness – it made me drop on my knees beside the bed and seize once more the chance of possessing him. "Dear little Miles, dear little Miles, if you knew how I want to help you! It's only that, it's nothing but that, and I'd rather die than give you a pain or do you a wrong – I'd rather die than hurt a hair of you. Dear little Miles" – oh, I brought it out now even if I should go too far – "I just want you to help me to save you!" But I knew in a moment after this that I had gone too far. (17.25)

Thought: Anyone as tightly wound as the Governess is bound to explode sometime. Here, we see the first of her explosions – her outburst towards Miles demonstrates her desire not simply to *save* him, as she suggests to him, but instead to *possess* him, a much more violent (and interestingly, rather Quint-ian) idea.

It was Flora who, gazing all over me in candid wonder, was the first. She was struck with our bareheaded aspect. "Why, where are your things?"

"Where yours are, my dear!" I promptly returned.

She had already got back her gaiety, and appeared to take this as an answer quite sufficient, "And where's Miles?" she went on.

There was something in the small valor of it that quite finished me: these three words from her were, in a flash like the glitter of a drawn blade, the jostle of the cup that my hand, for weeks and weeks, had held high and full to the brim and that now, even before speaking, I felt overflow in a deluge. "I'll tell you if you'll tell me – –" I heard myself say, then heard the tremor in which it broke.

"Well, what?"

Mrs. Grose's suspense blazed at me, but it was too late now, and I brought the thing out handsomely. "Where, my pet, is Miss Jessel?" (19.6-9)

Thought: … And here we have explosion number two from the Governess. After hiding her suspicions for most of the summer, she finally goes through with the dramatic accusation she envisioned earlier, even though Mrs. Grose silently implores her not to, proving that we simply *can't* contain things internally forever.

While this was done Miles stood again with his hands in his little pockets and his back to me – stood and looked out of the wide window through which, that other day, I had seen what pulled me up. We continued silent while the maid was with us – as silent, it whimsically occurred to me, as some young couple who, on their wedding journey, at the inn, feel shy in the presence of the waiter. He turned round only when the waiter had left us. "Well – so we're alone!" (22.5)

Thought: OK, ick. The sexual tension between the boy and his teacher is unbearably uncomfortable – yet, like all hints of sexuality in this text, it goes unmentioned, which makes it even less comfortable for readers. Miles's statement, "We're alone!" paired with the bridal imagery, makes us wonder unpleasantly what's going through the Governess's mind, that even she might not recognize.

Society and Class Quotes

The scene had a greatness that made it a different affair from my own scant home, and there immediately appeared at the door, with a little girl in her hand, a civil person who dropped me as decent a curtsy as if I had been the mistress or a distinguished visitor. I had received in Harley Street a narrower notion of the place, and that, as I recalled it, made me think the proprietor still more of a gentleman, suggested that what I was to enjoy might be something beyond his promise. (1.1)

Thought: Part of the appeal of Bly is the notion of escaping one's class and playing at wealth – we see it here in the Governess, and, in an interesting common trait, we see it in Peter Quint later.

I used to speculate – but even this with a dim disconnectedness – as to how the rough future (for all futures are rough!) would handle them and might bruise them. They had the bloom of health and happiness; and yet, as if I had been in charge of a pair of little grandees, of princes of the blood, for whom everything, to be right, would have to be enclosed and protected, the only form that, in my fancy, the afteryears could take for them was that of a romantic, a really royal extension of the garden and the park. (3.8)

Thought: The children are consistently set above everyone else; we don't know what the actual social status of the family is, but they're certainly of a different breed, so to speak, than the rest of the characters.

It lasted while I just bridled a little with the sense that my office demanded that there should be no such ignorance and no such person. It lasted while this visitant, at all events – and there was a touch of the strange freedom, as I remember, in the sign of familiarity of his wearing no hat – seemed to fix me, from his position, with just the question, just the scrutiny through the fading light, that his own presence provoked. (3.12)

Thought: Both the Governess and her "visitant," Quint, are perhaps a little too familiar with the house – she makes a big fuss about how he's not wearing a hat, while at the same time, she assumes that she already has the right to know everyone and everything about Bly.

She thought a minute. "Was he a gentleman?"

I found I had no need to think. "No." She gazed in deeper wonder. "No."

"Then nobody about the place? Nobody from the village?"

"Nobody – nobody. I didn't tell you, but I made sure."

She breathed a vague relief: this was, oddly, so much to the good. It only went indeed a little way, "But if he isn't a gentleman –"

"What is he? He's a horror."

"A horror?"

"He's – God help me if I know what he is!" (5.9-11)

Thought: Interesting – apparently, the only options for social status are either a "gentleman" or a "horror" in this context. Does that make all people of a lower social status "horrors?"

"Oh, it wasn't him!" Mrs. Grose with emphasis declared. "It was Quint's own fancy. To play with him, I mean – to spoil him," She paused a moment; then she added: "Quint was much too free."

This gave me, straight from my vision of his face – such a face! – a sudden sickness of disgust. "Too free with my boy?"

"Too free with everyone!" (6.8-9)

Thought: It becomes clear that the real source of Quint's evil was his inability to stick to the limitations of his class – Mrs. Grose, who certainly knows her place and stays there adamantly, doesn't approve of the liberties he took with all the members of the household when he was in charge, playing lord of the manor.

So, for a little, we faced it once more together; and I found absolutely a degree of help in seeing it now so straight. "I appreciate," I said, "the great decency of your not having hitherto spoken; but the time has certainly come to give me the whole thing." She appeared to assent to this, but still only in silence; seeing which I went on: "I must have it now. Of what did she die? Come, there was something between them."

"There was everything."

"In spite of the difference – ?"

"Oh, of their rank, their condition" – she brought it woefully out. "She was a lady."

I turned it over; I again saw. "Yes – she was a lady."

"And he so dreadfully below," said Mrs. Grose.

I felt that I doubtless needn't press too hard, in such company, on the place of a servant in the scale; but there was nothing to prevent an acceptance of my companion's own measure of my predecessor's abasement. There was a way to deal with that, and I dealt; the more readily for my full vision – on the evidence – of our employer's late clever, good-looking "own" man; impudent, assured, spoiled, depraved. "The fellow was a hound."

Mrs. Grose considered as if it were perhaps a little a case for a sense of shades. "I've never seen one like him. He did what he wished."

"With her?"

"With them all." (7.18-20)

Thought: Again, Mrs. Grose ominously indicates that Quint was, as she says earlier, "too free" with everyone – particularly Miss Jessel. Their cross-class romantic relationship is one of the central disturbances of this story; the Governess, who, whether she likes it or not, identifies in a way with Miss Jessel, is both revolted and fascinated by the "abasement" of the previous governess.

I drew a great security in this particular from [Mrs. Grose's] mere smooth aspect. There was nothing in her fresh face to pass on to others my horrible confidences. She believed me, I was sure, absolutely: if she hadn't I don't know what would have become of me, for I couldn't have borne the business alone. But she was a magnificent monument to the blessing of a want of imagination, and if she could see in our little charges nothing but their beauty and amiability, their happiness and cleverness, she had no direct communication with the sources of my trouble. If they had been at all visibly blighted or battered, she would doubtless have grown, on tracing it back, haggard enough to match them; as matters stood, however, I could feel her, when she surveyed them, with her large white arms folded and the habit of serenity in all her look, thank the Lord's mercy that if they were ruined the pieces would still serve. (11.1)

Thought: Unlike Quint and Miss Jessel (and perhaps the Governess herself), Mrs. Grose is the ideal hired help – she knows exactly what the limitations of her job and rank are, and she doesn't even think about stretching beyond them. She is also apparently exceptionally unimaginative, and takes everything at face value, from the Governess's claims to the children's innocence.

Mrs. Grose watched them with positive placidity; then I caught the suppressed intellectual creak with which she conscientiously turned to take from me a view of the back of the tapestry. I had made her a receptacle of lurid things, but there was an odd recognition of my superiority – my accomplishments and my function – in her patience under my pain. She offered her mind to my disclosures as, had I wished to mix a witch's broth and proposed it with assurance, she would have held out a large clean saucepan. (11.2)

Thought: Again, good old Mrs. Grose shows us just how amenable she is to abiding by class definitions– though the Governess basically just keeps filling her mind with rather poisonous thoughts, she keeps accepting them, perhaps largely because she acknowledges the superiority of the Governess's office – and therefore her supposed superiority as a person.

Seated at my own table in clear noonday light I saw a person whom without my previous experience I should have taken at the first blush for some housemaid who might have stayed at home to look after the place and who, availing herself of rare relief from observation and of the schoolroom table and my pens, ink, and paper, had applied herself to the considerable effort of a letter to her sweetheart. (15.5)

Thought: Though we know that Miss Jessel is/was a "lady," here she is compared to a servant writing a love letter. This implies that a different moral code might be applied to the working classes – it's all right for a mere maid to have a sweetheart somewhere, but it was *not* OK for Miss Jessel and Quint to have a relationship. We wonder if this image also plays upon the Governess's own desires to have a sweetheart somewhere to write to.

Wisdom and Knowledge Quotes

I hesitated; then I judged best simply to hand her my letter – which, however, had the effect of making her, without taking it, simply put her hands behind her. She shook her head sadly. "Such things are not for me, miss."

My counselor couldn't read! I winced at my mistake, which I attenuated as I could, and opened my letter again to repeat it to her. (2.5)

Thought: Mrs. Grose's illiteracy introduces the idea that some types of learning or knowledge are not for everyone.

I was lifted aloft on a great wave of infatuation and pity. I found it simple, in my ignorance, my confusion, and perhaps my conceit, to assume that I could deal with a boy whose education for the world was all on the point of beginning. I am unable even to remember at this day what proposal I framed for the end of his holidays and the resumption of his studies. Lessons with me, indeed, that charming summer, we all had a theory that he was to have; but I now feel that, for weeks, the lessons must have been rather my own. I learned something – at first, certainly – that had not been one of the teachings of my small, smothered life; learned to be amused, and even amusing, and not to think for the morrow. It was the first time, in a manner, that I had known space and air and freedom, all the music of summer and all the mystery of nature. And then there was consideration – and consideration was sweet. Oh, it was a trap – not designed, but deep – to my imagination, to my delicacy, perhaps to my vanity; to whatever, in me, was most excitable. The best way to picture it all is to say that I was off my guard. (3.8)

Thought: Here, we see the teacher become the student – the Governess ends up learning from her pupils how to enjoy day-to-day life…but is it simply a diversion? Can this new "knowledge" really be a distraction?

The flash of this knowledge – for it was knowledge in the midst of dread – produced in me the most extraordinary effect, started, as I stood there, a sudden vibration of duty and courage. I say courage because I was beyond all doubt already far gone. I bounded straight out of the

door again, reached that of the house, got in an instant, upon the drive, and, passing along the terrace as fast as I could rush, turned a corner and came full in sight. But it was in sight of nothing now – my visitor had vanished. (4.6)

Thought: The Governess is constantly having these "flashes" of insight, particularly with regards to the ghosts – how? Why? We never get a satisfactory explanation for how she "knows" things.

"He was looking for someone else, you say – someone who was not you?"

"He was looking for little Miles." A portentous clearness now possessed me. "That's whom he was looking for."

"But how do you know?"

"I know, I know, I know!" My exaltation grew. "And you know, my dear!" (6.3)

Thought: Again, the Governess's mysterious certainty rears its puzzling head. She demonstrates a certain triumph, or, as she calls it, "exaltation," which could perhaps be explained as the thrill of certainty, even without proof.

She felt my discrimination. "I daresay I was wrong. But, really, I was afraid."

"Afraid of what?"

"Of things that man could do. Quint was so clever – he was so deep." (6.10)

Thought: Hmm... you have to wonder what exactly James means when he uses the word "deep." Clearly it's not a good thing – but it's also not entirely a bad thing. Does it simply mean "intelligent" or "cunning," or is there another implication at work here?

I was there to protect and defend the little creatures in the world the most bereaved and the most lovable, the appeal of whose helplessness had suddenly become only too explicit, a deep, constant ache of one's own committed heart. We were cut off, really, together; we were united in our danger. They had nothing but me, and I – well, I had them. It was in short a magnificent chance. This chance presented itself to me in an image richly material. I was a screen – I was to stand before them. The more I saw, the less they would. (6.13)

Thought: This is a majorly important quote in the story – it's basically the Governess's mission statement. Her assertion that she'll absorb all the bad things aimed at the children is both a self-sacrificing gesture and an oddly pleasurable, anticipatory one…the Governess relishes new knowledge so much that we wonder if she might actually enjoy this duty.

I got hold of Mrs. Grose as soon after this as I could; and I can give no intelligible account of how I fought out the interval. Yet I still hear myself cry as I fairly threw myself into her arms: "They know – it's too monstrous: they know, they know!"

"And what on earth – ?" I felt her incredulity as she held me.

"Why, all that we know – and heaven knows what else besides!" (7.1)

Thought: The worst possible threat, apparently, is not just that the children might know as much as the adults – but that they might know *more*. Gasp!

"No, no – there are depths, depths! The more I go over it, the more I see in it, and the more I see in it, the more I fear. I don't know what I don't see – what I don't fear!" (7.7)

Thought: Again with the depths, huh? Everything in this story has depths – they perhaps represent sinkholes of knowledge, things that one can never really understand or know everything about.

"[…] Oh, yes, we may sit here and look at them, and they may show off to us there to their fill; but even while they pretend to be lost in their fairytale they're steeped in their vision of the dead restored. He's not reading to her," I declared; "they're talking of them – they're talking horrors! I go on, I know, as if I were crazy; and it's a wonder I'm not. What I've seen would have made you so; but it has only made me more lucid, made me get hold of still other things." (12.1)

Thought: Here, the Governess presents the odd and rather condescending idea that the knowledge that she has gained and the things that she's experienced have only made her stronger and helped her see clearer, but could have destroyed somebody else (like, for example, Mrs. Grose).

"She's there, you little unhappy thing – there, there, there, and you see her as well as you see me!" I had said shortly before to Mrs. Grose that she was not at these times a child, but an old, old woman, and that description of her could not have been more strikingly confirmed than in the way in which, for all answer to this, she simply showed me, without an expressional concession or admission, a countenance of deeper and deeper, of indeed suddenly quite fixed, reprobation. (20.2)

Thought: In this moment, we're not sure who knows what – does the Governess really know that Flora can see Miss Jessel? *Can* Flora really see her? Or does Flora know that the Governess is totally insane?

Gender Quotes

This person proved, on her presenting herself, for judgment, at a house in Harley Street, that impressed her as vast and imposing – this prospective patron proved a gentleman, a bachelor in the prime of life, such a figure as had never risen, save in a dream or an old novel, before a fluttered, anxious girl out of a Hampshire vicarage. One could easily fix this type; it never, happily, dies out. He was handsome and bold and pleasant, offhand and gay and kind. He struck her, inevitably, as gallant and splendid, but what took her most of all and gave her the courage she afterward showed was that he put the whole thing to her as a kind of favor, an obligation he should gratefully incur. She conceived him as rich, but as fearfully extravagant – saw him all in a glow of high fashion, of good looks, of expensive habits, of charming ways with women. (Prologue.13)

Thought: The overwhelming manliness of the Governess's employer is his most outstanding feature – he's really a very generic, undetailed, impersonal rich man as far as we can tell. However, this is enough to win over the Governess from the moment she meets him.

"Well, that, I think, is what I came for – to be carried away. I'm afraid, however," I remember feeling the impulse to add, "I'm rather easily carried away. I was carried away in London!"

I can still see Mrs. Grose's broad face as she took this in. "In Harley Street?"

"In Harley Street."

"Well, miss, you're not the first – and you won't be the last." (1.6-7)

Thought: This brief exchange comments upon the implicitly female tendency to be "carried away" by men (Miles is referenced beforehand).

"I take what you said to me at noon as a declaration that you've never known him to be bad."

She threw back her head; she had clearly, by this time, and very honestly, adopted an attitude. "Oh, never known him – I don't pretend that!"

I was upset again. "Then you have known him — ?"

"Yes indeed, miss, thank God!"

On reflection I accepted this. "You mean that a boy who never is — ?"

"Is no boy for me!" (2.12-15)

Thought: Boys are here given more leeway than girls; while Flora is expected to be flawless, Mrs. Grose admits that she *wants* Miles to be a little naughty.

An unknown man in a lonely place is a permitted object of fear to a young woman privately bred; and the figure that faced me was – a few more seconds assured me – as little anyone else I knew as it was the image that had been in my mind. (3.11)

Thought: The tension between the "unknown man" and the Governess is palpable, even at a great distance (remember, he's standing atop a tower, and doesn't pose an immediate threat to her). This perspective on the relationship of men and women implies the threat of violence at any time.

I had had brothers myself, and it was no revelation to me that little girls could be slavish idolaters of little boys. What surpassed everything was that there was a little boy in the world who could have for the inferior age, sex, and intelligence so fine a consideration. They were extraordinarily at one, and to say that they never either quarreled or complained is to make the note of praise coarse for their quality of sweetness. (9.3)

Thought: Miles and Flora's unique relationship is sweet on one hand, but a little *too* sweet on the other, if you ask us. The phrasing of this description comes off as condescending to our contemporary ears (we have to remember that this was the common view of the status of men in relation to women in James's day), and we wonder for the umpteenth time if Miles is really as swell as he seems to be.

Turned out for Sunday by his uncle's tailor, who had had a free hand and a notion of pretty waistcoats and of his grand little air, Miles's whole title to independence, the rights of his sex and situation, were so stamped upon him that if he had suddenly struck for freedom I should have had nothing to say. I was by the strangest of chances wondering how I should meet him when the revolution unmistakably occurred. (14.1)

Thought: Miles and the Governess are sitting on an odd metaphorical seesaw – the question is, when does a woman in an authority position get outweighed by a male child, who has more heft simply because of his gender?

"I want my own sort!"

It literally made me bound forward. "There are not many of your own sort, Miles!" I laughed. "Unless perhaps dear little Flora!"

"You really compare me to a baby girl?" (14.12)

Thought: Ah *ha* – finally we see Miles betray some inner tension. While the Governess rather naively thinks that Miles and his sister are equals because of their birth and status, Miles's bitter reply shows that he rates them on different levels – by deriding Flora as a "baby girl," he claims superiority not just by age, but by gender.

Literature and Writing Quotes

"I quite agree – in regard to Griffin's ghost, or whatever it was – that its appearing first to the little boy, at so tender an age, adds a particular touch. But it's not the first occurrence of its charming kind that I know to have involved a child. If the child gives the effect another turn of the screw, what do you say to two children –?"

"We say, of course," somebody exclaimed, "that they give two turns! Also that we want to hear about them." (Prologue.2)

Thought: From the beginning, this story is all about the writer and/or narrator. We're very conscious of the fact that we're being told a story, and that it's carefully constructed by someone. This "turn of the screw" conversation loosely compares the crafting of the story to building something with one's hands, highlighting the image of the writer as a craftsman.

I can see Douglas there before the fire, to which he had got up to present his back, looking down at his interlocutor with his hands in his pockets. "Nobody but me, till now, has ever heard. It's quite too horrible." This, naturally, was declared by several voices to give the thing the utmost price, and our friend, with quiet art, prepared his triumph by turning his eyes over the rest of us and going on: "It's beyond everything. Nothing at all that I know touches it." (Prologue.3)

Thought: These preliminary scenes serve two purposes; firstly, they tell a little story of their own (that of Douglas and the governess), and secondly, they steadily increase the reader's curiosity and anticipation, along with those of Douglas's audience.

So far had Douglas presented his picture when someone put a question. "And what did the former governess die of? – of so much respectability?"

Our friend's answer was prompt. "That will come out. I don't anticipate."

"Excuse me – I thought that was just what you are doing." (Prologue.15-16)

Thought: Here, one of the guests comments aptly upon Douglas's steady buildup of the story before it even begins; this could be seen as a playful comment upon the rather heavy-handed devices of suspense so often employed by authors of the genre.

"What is your title?"

"I haven't one."

"Oh, I have!" I said. (Prologue.18)

Thought: Again, we're reminded that this is a piece of writing – the Prologue's narrator is clearly a writer (we know that it is actually he who published this story, supposedly), and he's always thinking in terms of literary construction.

It may be, of course, above all, that what suddenly broke into this gives the previous time a charm of stillness – that hush in which something gathers or crouches. The change was actually like the spring of a beast. (3.8)

Thought: Wow, foreshadow much? The Governess has a way of leaving us with little mini-cliffhangers; she warns us every time things are about to get worse. This is a profoundly literary strategy – it builds reader anticipation skillfully, without being too heavy-handed or giving things away early.

It was not that I didn't wait, on this occasion, for more, for I was rooted as deeply as I was shaken. Was there a "secret" at Bly – a mystery of Udolpho or an insane, an unmentionable relative kept in unsuspected confinement? (4.1)

Thought: Interestingly, the first references that spring to mind when the Governess sees Quint from afar are literary ones; this keeps the story within a certain literary framework and recalls the genre of gothic horror.

I find that I really hang back; but I must take my plunge. In going on with the record of what was hideous at Bly, I not only challenge the most liberal faith – for which I little care; but – and this is another matter – I renew what I myself suffered, I again push my way through it to the end. (9.4)

Thought: Here, the Governess acknowledges the documentary nature of her task – even though it pains her, she forces herself to keep writing to the end.

Would exasperation, however, if relief had longer been postponed, finally have betrayed me? It little matters, for relief arrived. I call it relief, though it was only the relief that a snap brings to a strain or the burst of a thunderstorm to a day of suffocation. It was at least change, and it came with a rush. (13.4)

Thought: The Governess really has a way with catchy chapter endings – she gives hints at what is to come, but refuses to give away more (except the constant implication that what's coming is *really bad*). This strategy is what makes the story *obviously* a short story, not a personal manuscript as we are meant to believe; in this clear structure, we can see the hand of the fiction writer behind all of this, despite its pose as a kind of testimony.

Plot Analysis

Classic Plot Analysis

Initial Situation

The Governess arrives on the scene at Bly (Chapter One)
The beginning of the story is set up very neatly for us; first, Douglas gives us the critical background information on the Governess in the Prologue, then we immediately see her arrive at Bly, ready to start her job.

Conflict

The Governess receives a letter from Miles's school (via her employer in London) saying that the boy has been expelled and can never return (Chapter Two)
This development throws a wrench in the lovely little life the Governess has started to construct at Bly with Flora. She wonders what the boy could possibly have done to merit expulsion – what could be so bad that the headmaster couldn't even explain it in his letter home?

Complication

The mysterious male figure appears atop the tower, then at the dining room window; the Governess and Mrs. Grose talk about the dead servant, Peter Quint (Chapters Three - Five)
The tension builds as the Governess is haunted by the odd, out of place figure she sees on the tower; when she sees him again through the dining room window, she's flat-out terrified. The real complication here is not just that the figure is identified as the rascal Peter Quint – it's that Quint is *dead*.

Climax

Miss Jessel appears by the lake for the first time – can it be that Flora's lying? (Chapters Six - Seven)
Upon seeing the ghost that she's convinced is Miss Jessel, the Governess has a horrible revelation: she thinks the children, or at least Flora, are working together with the ghosts. This first appearance of doubt about the innocence of the children is what sparks the rest of the plot.

Suspense

Nighttime wanderings create more suspicion… (Chapters Ten - Eleven)
This time, both of the children are involved in sketchy dealings; the Governess first discovers Flora out of bed, looking out at the lawn. Days later, she finds both the children in compromising positions, with Flora at the window again and Miles hanging out outside (possibly looking up at Quint, who may or may not be atop the tower again). The Governess's suspicions worsen.

Denouement

Two options: Flora's guilt is confirmed by her denial of seeing Miss Jessel, OR the Governess's madness is confirmed because nobody else can see the ghost (Chapters Nineteen - Twenty)
Mrs. Grose and the Governess discover Flora by the lake, and the Governess flat out accuses

the girl of seeing the dead governess. Flora's denial can mean one of two things – either the girl is lying, thereby confirming the Governess's suspicions, *or* the Governess is a total loon, which could be confirmed by the fact that neither Flora nor Mrs. Grose can see Miss Jessel.

Conclusion
Quint reappears a last time; Miles dies (Chapter Twenty-Four)
Well, this ending doesn't actually "conclude" anything, but it *does* provide us with a provocative and rather sudden final event. The story, as far as we're concerned, can't possibly go on past this point, since Quint evidently disappears and Miles abruptly dies. Mrs. Grose and Flora are also out of the picture, doing who knows what in London, so we're just left with what we started with – the Governess, alone, and questionably trustworthy.

Booker's Seven Basic Plots Analysis: Tragedy

Anticipation Stage
The Prologue
So, as you've probably noticed, this is a rather unconventional story. A large part of the story's thrill comes from the experience of reading, rather than the actual events of the tale. This begins with the very first few pages of the piece; the Narrator and Douglas both build up the tension in the "audience" of listeners at the house party, which also serves to create a sense of anxiety for us, the readers.

Dream Stage
The Governess takes up residence at Bly, and is infatuated by her students and by her new life on the whole. (Chapters One – Three)
Life looks like a big bowl of Victorian cherries for the first few chapters of this book; though there are minor complications, like Miles's mysterious dismissal from school, but the Governess is willing to overlook these things. She's too busy being infatuated with the two angelic children, who are, simply put, too good to be true. It's summer and everything is idyllic; the world seems like a pretty good place…for now, at least.

Frustration Stage
Peter Quint's appearance on the tower, and his return (up close and personal) outside the window. (End of Chapter Three)
True to "Tragedy" form, a shadow figure appears at the end of Chapter 3. Peter Quint's introduction sparks this stage of the story, in which suspicions begin to build about Quint, about the children, and about the recent history of Bly in general.

Nightmare Stage
The Governess suspects that Flora saw Miss Jessel and lied. (Chapter Seven)
For the first time, the innocence of the children is really thrown into question. The Governess actually breaks down at the end of Chapter Seven, fearing that it's too late to save the children at all, and that the ghosts have already won. Little does she know that things at Bly are only going to get worse…much, much worse.

Destruction/Death Wish Stage

Flora denies seeing the ghost; the Governess decides to cast the girl aside and focus on "saving" Miles. (Chapter Nineteen – Chapter Twenty-Four)

After Flora's breakdown and accusation of the Governess, the "Destruction" stage sets in; the Governess cuts her losses and abandons Flora, choosing to try and salvage Miles instead of both siblings. The Governess's obsession with the boy reaches its peak here, and her fervor to force him to confess his transgressions is what pushes the story to its tragic conclusion. She goes all out in trying to "save" the boy, but, in the end, doesn't succeed.

Three Act Plot Analysis

Act I

The short-lived idyll of the Governess's new life at Bly ends abruptly with the unsettling first two appearances of Peter Quint – we know that something's *majorly* wrong when Mrs. Grose reveals that Quint is actually dead.

Act II

Though there are various moments of despair in this story, the first and most significant is the Governess's revelation that Flora is involved with the ghosts (provoked by her first glimpse of Miss Jessel at the lake); here, she worries that it's too late to save the children, and that they're already lost.

Act III

The third act begins with the Governess's suspicion of the children, and builds up towards the super-dramatic ending – Miles's death.

Study Questions

1. In your opinion, are the ghosts real, or are they manifestations of the Governess's imagination?
2. What exactly is so scary about Peter Quint (well, aside from the fact that he's dead)?
3. Why are the Governess and Mrs. Grose so disturbed by the idea that the children might know about the illicit relationship between Miss Jessel and Peter Quint?
4. What, if anything, do you think the ghosts are trying to do to the children?
5. Why does Miles die?

Characters

All Characters

The Governess Character Analysis

The Governess is the only character we can really sink our teeth into in this story, and boy, is it worth it. She's a truly fascinating character; we're never quite sure how trustworthy she is as a narrator, but at least she never fails to keep us on our toes.

As for the facts, they are relatively few and far between: we know that she's only twenty years old, and that she's the daughter of a poor country parson. She's clearly something of a romantic, at least at the beginning, and this inclination contributes to her acceptance of the job at Bly. Though she only meets her employer twice, she's sufficiently swept off her feet, and spends the rest of the story secretly in love (or something approximating it) with him.

Now that we've got the easy stuff out of the way, it's time to tackle the more complicated elements of the Governess's personality. There are traditionally two ways of viewing her character – as either a sane heroine or a insane anti-heroine. Both sides have passionate adherents; if you ever want to pick a nasty fight in a room full of English majors, bring up *The Turn of the Screw*. Let's take a look at both of these cases – we leave the final verdict up to all of you.

How could you doubt her? The Governess is totally sane.
The classic reading of this story is that we assume that our heroine to be in full possession of her mental faculties (that is, she's not crazy), and that all of these supernatural things actually take place in the real world. This view of the Governess places her in the role of the traditional heroine, and assumes that she is really acting for the good of the children; it also assumes that the children are in fact in cahoots with the ghostly visitors, and that both Flora and Miles are little deceivers.

If we are to look at things this way, then we see the Governess as a strong-willed, intelligent, and noble young woman, who ultimately ends up a victim of Quint and Jessel, as do the two children.

Don't trust her! The Governess is a madwoman.
The most popular alternate reading of the character is that the Governess is 100% certifiably insane, and that the supernatural activity is all a manifestation of her tormented, repressed mental state. This psychoanalytic perspective was first proposed by the influential literary critic Edmund Wilson, in a 1938 essay entitled "The Ambiguity of Henry James." In the essay, Wilson carefully lays out several instances in which he sees signs of Freudian symbolism in the story; the Governess stands out as a neurotic, sexually repressed woman, whose hidden desires drive her mad. Wilson's essay generated a whole lot of conversation around the story, which has always been one of James's most oft-discussed works.

The Governess Timeline and Summary

- The Governess, rather overwhelmed by her interview with the gentleman at Harley Street, accepts the Bly job offer.
- She travels to Bly, and is pleasantly surprised by the impressive house and its surroundings.
- The Governess is also pleased with Mrs. Grose and Flora; she's particularly impressed by the little girl's angelic looks.
- The Governess thinks she hears some creepy activity in the house that night, but ignores it.
- Things go well for the first few days; the Governess tries to get to know Flora better, and can't wait to see what Miles is like.
- The Governess receives a letter from Miles's school, via his uncle, who's uninterested. The letter requests that Miles never return.
- Mrs. Grose tries to convince the Governess that Miles could never possibly be bad enough to be expelled from school – this makes the Governess even more curious about the boy.
- The Governess tries to learn more about her predecessor, but hits a conversational brick wall with Mrs. Grose.
- When Miles arrives, the Governess is immediately won over by his adorable little face and his air of purity.
- Everything goes swimmingly for a while – the Governess loves her pupils and her job.
- One day, while walking and daydreaming of meeting a man, she *does* encounter a man – but not one that she wants to meet. She sees a mysterious figure on top of one of the house's towers, gazing at her malevolently.
- The Governess is nervous that perhaps Bly has some terrible secret.
- Despite this unsettling encounter, the Governess cheers up in the company of her pupils.
- One Sunday, the Governess has a second encounter with the evil mystery man – this time, he's looking in the window of the dining room at her, but she has the feeling that he's looking for someone else.
- She goes outside to investigate the stranger. While she's out there, Mrs. Grose sees her from inside, and is terrified.
- It emerges that the man the Governess has seen is Peter Quint – and that he's dead.
- The Governess finally gets some background info on what went on at Bly before her arrival; she's proud to defend her two charges against the evil influence of Quint.
- The Governess takes it upon herself to block the children from any harm – she starts to watch them obsessively.
- One day, playing by the lake, another mysterious figure appears – this time it's a woman, who appears to be equally evil.
- The Governess thinks that Flora has seen the ghostly woman, but has pretended not to. She spills the beans to Mrs. Grose, seeking advice.
- The Governess is sure she knows who this second spirit is – Miss Jessel, her predecessor.
- Now that Flora has been implicated in the Governess's mind, she's worried about what happens when she's *not* watching the children – are they communing with the ghosts?

- The Governess breaks down and cries, worrying that it's too late to save the children.
- Mrs. Grose and the Governess attempt to keep their cool and solve this ghostly problem.
- The Governess doesn't worry about herself, and instead claims that she's only worried about keeping the children safe.
- The Governess does some further research, pumping Mrs. Grose for information. She finds out that Miles and Quint spent a lot of time together, despite the fact that Mrs. Grose didn't approve, and that Miss Jessel thought it was all fine and dandy.
- The Governess says that she's not accusing anyone of anything, and that she has to keep watching the children.
- She waits it out for a little while; she and the children are unusually cheerful and affectionate with each other. She's afraid that she might give away some of her suspicions to them.
- One night, the Governess has a feeling that something's disturbing the house; she leaves her room and goes out into the hall, where she encounters Quint on the staircase. She's not scared this time – they simply regard each other silently. Quint disappears.
- Returning to her room, the Governess discovers that Flora is out of bed; it turns out she's looking out the window, and is hidden behind a curtain. The Governess puts the child back to bed, but secretly wonders what she was up to.
- After this episode, the Governess patrols the hallways at night, perhaps hoping to encounter the ghost again. She doesn't see Quint, but she does see the specter of Miss Jessel on the same staircase.
- On the eleventh night after the Quint sighting, the Governess discovers that Flora has left her bed again, and is looking at something out the same window. The Governess sneaks out of their room, seeking a window that looks out onto whatever Flora's gazing at.
- On her way, she stops and eavesdrops at Miles's door for a moment – it's totally silent.
- Upon finding another window, the Governess looks out and sees a figure, who's looking up at someone else on top of the tower. The figure on the lawn is *not* Miss Jessel, as expected – it's Miles!
- The Governess relates the story to Mrs. Grose the next day, and we find out what happened next – she went out to fetch Miles, and he came willingly. His reason for going out in the night was apparently to prove that he can be bad. Hmm…
- The Governess is even more convinced that the children are communing with Quint and Jessel. She's sure that the ghosts intend to lure the children to their deaths somehow.
- Mrs. Grose suggests that the Governess write to the children's uncle to tell him about what's happening, which she refuses to do – after all, she promised him that she would never contact him, and she doesn't want to let him down. She threatens to leave if the housekeeper summons him.
- Another month passes without any supernatural activity; tensions are rising with the Governess and her charges, though, and she constantly has to keep herself from bringing up the two dead servants. She privately rehearses what she would say if she were to confront the kids.
- Miles confronts the Governess about his return to school – he feels like he's missing out on life by staying at Bly, and forcefully says that he wants to be with people like him.
- The Governess, shaken by this scene with Miles, decides that she has to leave Bly – immediately. She runs home to pack her things. In a moment of indecision, she collapses on the stairs exactly where she saw Miss Jessel.
- In the schoolroom, the Governess sees Miss Jessel once more. This time, the ghost

makes her feel like an intruder in her own classroom. She angrily confronts the ghost, who makes no reply, and simply disappears.

- The Governess decides to stay at Bly.
- The Governess tells Mrs. Grose about her encounter with Miss Jessel, but adds more on – she claims that the two of them spoke, and that the ghost told the Governess that she suffers the torments of damnation.
- The Governess resolves to tell the children's uncle about everything.
- The Governess and Miles have an awkward, rather sketchy encounter in Miles's room late one night – she attempts to learn more about his school days, but he refuses to tell her.
- Desperate, the Governess begs Miles to let her save him. There's immediately a seemingly supernatural response in the room; it's battered by cold winds, despite the fact that the window is closed.
- The candle is extinguished – Miles says that he blew it out.
- The Governess writes the letter to the children's uncle, but doesn't post it.
- While Miles distracts the Governess, Flora disappears; the two women go in search of her.
- The women find Flora at the lake. The Governess finally comes out and confronts Flora, asking where Miss Jessel is. She then sees the ghost of Miss Jessel across the water and alerts Flora and Mrs. Grose – both of them deny seeing it. Flora freaks out and denies that she ever saw anything, and wants to get away from the Governess.
- When she returns to the house, Flora is nowhere to be seen, but Miles comes to keep her company.
- The Governess is certain that Flora is lying. She tells Mrs. Grose to take Flora to London to see her uncle, while she herself will try and win Miles over.
- According to Mrs. Grose, the Governess's letter never made it to town – she thinks that Miles stole it.
- Miles and the Governess have an awkward dinner together, after which she confronts him about the letter.
- The Governess sees Peter Quint's terrible face outside the window once more, and she struggles to keep Miles from seeing him.
- Miles admits to having taken the letter – furthermore, we finally find out that he was asked to leave school because he "said things" (we're not sure what, and he won't say) to other students.
- In desperation, the Governess yells out to Quint. Miles, in a rush of emotion, asks if Miss Jessel is there.
- The Governess cries out that it's not Miss Jessel, it's another. Miles guesses that it's Peter Quint.
- The Governess clutches at the boy, trying to tell him that Quint doesn't matter anymore, since he belongs to *her* now.
- Miles looks to the window, but sees nothing. In relief, the Governess clutches him to her, but realizes that the boy has died.

Miles Character Analysis

For a character as central as Miles is, we actually know very little about him – which is actually

what makes him so mystifying and interesting. Some might complain about the comparatively small number of characters we really get to know in this story (the number hovers somewhere between one and zero – after all, *can* we really say we "know" the Governess?). But we at Shmoop think that this odd distance from the actors in the story is what creates its *Unsolved Mysteries*-style appeal.

What we do know about Miles is this: he's ten, he's frighteningly smart and impossibly beautiful, and he's strangely savvy in the ways of the world – think about the ten year old boys *you* know, and Miles's precocity becomes strikingly apparent. We also know that he may or may not have the capacity to be incredibly bad; his schoolmasters declare that he's so wicked he can't even come back to school.

The cause of Miles's expulsion is one of the central mysteries in the plot; we find out at the end that he was kicked out merely for saying things, but it's up to us to imagine what he possibly could have said to other students that would merit such a punishment. One popular speculation on the nature of Miles's transgression is that he made comments of a homosexual nature to some of his fellow students – those that, as he says, he "liked." Whatever his punishable acts may be, this additional unknown only adds to the suspense and the intrigue of the story.

Speaking of unknowns, there's the matter of Miles's death. His last words are mysterious: he calls out "Peter Quint – you devil!" (24.24). We're not sure if he's referring to Quint as a devil or the governess herself. Furthermore, we don't know why Miles dies. It's possibly because the spirit of Quint leaves him, possibly because of the shock of all this uproar…and possibly (dare we say it?) because the Governess herself harms him…It's a mystery. And James clearly knew that what we as readers can *imagine* is vastly more frightening and haunting than what he, the author, could have ever committed to the page.

Miles Timeline and Summary

- Miles returns to Bly for the summer after school lets out.
- Miles succeeds in effortlessly charming the Governess with his sweet nature and good looks.
- Everything goes well for our little faux-family unit of Miles, Flora, and the Governess – for a little while, at least.
- After the ghosts appear, the Governess discovers, unbeknownst to Miles, that he and Quint had a close relationship – something he notably never mentions.
- The night of the second Flora-at-the-window incident, the Governess discovers that Miles is the figure on the lawn that the girl is looking at.
- The Governess goes outside to fetch Miles. He excuses himself playfully, saying that he only wanted to show the Governess that he can be really bad when he wants to.
- Later on, Miles confronts the Governess about his supposed return to school, declaring that he can't just grow up in the country with a bunch of women.
- Miles declares that he wants to see more of life – and that he needs to be with people like him. We're not quite sure what he means by that.

- Miles demands that the Governess put the case before his uncle, thinking that the man will want him to go off to school again. He claims that he will make his uncle pay attention to them.
- The Governess and Miles have an awkward, rather sketchy encounter in Miles's room late one night – she attempts to learn more about his school days, but he refuses to tell her.
- Desperate, the Governess begs Miles to let her save him; there's immediately a seemingly supernatural response in the room – it's battered by cold winds, despite the fact that the window is closed.
- The candle is extinguished – Miles says that he blew it out. Again, we can't be sure what really happened…is he telling the truth?
- Miles lures the Governess away from Flora, and entertains her by playing music.
- While the second incident by the lake is going down, Miles runs off by himself and explores the grounds.
- After Flora and Mrs. Grose leave, Miles and the Governess are left alone. He tells her he's been enjoying his freedom.
- After one last dinner, the Governess confronts Miles about his past; he attempts to escape, saying that he needs to go see Luke, presumably a servant.
- The Governess demands to know if Miles took her letter to his uncle. He admits to it, saying that he found nothing of importance in it, and burned it.
- The truth about school finally emerges. Once Miles knows that the Governess knows "everything" about his expulsion, he finally confesses that he said some things to some of the students – interestingly, only those that he liked – and that the masters must have found out.
- Miles admits, when pressed, that some of these things must have been too bad to write home about.
- The Governess freaks out because of the reappearance of Peter Quint, and calls out to the ghost to go away. Miles, alarmed, asks if it's Miss Jessel.
- When the Governess tells him that it's *not* in fact the former governess, but is the other villain, Miles desperately turns to look at the ghost – but he's gone. As this is happening, he mysteriously calls out "Peter Quint – you devil!" (24.24).
- In relief that Peter Quint has disappeared, the Governess clutches Miles, but she discovers that he's dead in her arms.

Flora Character Analysis

Flora is two years younger than her brother (she's eight), and is just as adorable; the two of them are often compared to angels, and their beauty is their most prominent quality. Both of them seemingly cast a spell on the Governess just by merit of looking the way they do. Flora meets the Governess first, and though we don't see as much conversation between the two of them, we know that the little girl instantly wins the affection and adoration of her teacher. However, once Miles enters the scene, Flora kind of falls by the wayside.

If we know little about Miles, we know even less about Flora. Basically, all we get is that she's only slightly less compelling than her fabulous brother – and that, we might guess, is simply

because she's a girl. Miles's male-ness is what allows him to be forgiven time and time again by Mrs. Grose and the Governess, whereas Flora is the first to fall under suspicion. Notably, she's also dismissed by the Governess after the second lake incident, while the older woman stays with Miles to try and salvage him.

Flora Timeline and Summary

- Flora and Mrs. Grove meet the Governess when she arrives at Bly. She's instantly charmed by the child's good manners and, above all, her physical beauty.
- Flora gives the Governess a tour of the house.
- Playing by the lake, Flora may or may not see the figure of Miss Jessel appear – the Governess assumes that she does.
- The first night that the Governess leaves her room to prowl the halls, she returns and finds Flora gazing out the window; first, Flora turns the blame playfully upon the Governess, asking where *she* was. When asked, the girl says that she was worried when she awoke and found her roommate gone, and that she had a feeling that someone was outside.
- Several nights later, the Governess awakens mysteriously and again discovers that Flora is furtively out of bed and looking out the window – this time at Miles, who's on the lawn.
- Later on, as Miles distracts the Governess in the music room, Flora runs off. Mrs. Grose and the Governess discover her at the lake, where she has hidden the boat that's usually docked there.
- Flora tries to act as though nothing is wrong initially. However, the Governess can't control herself, and demands to know where Miss Jessel is.
- Flora freaks out, either because she's understandably frightened by the Governess, or because she's trying to act as though she doesn't know what's going on – as usual, we're not sure which interpretation to believe.
- Flora has a breakdown, and says that she never saw anyone, and that she just wants to get away from the Governess. Interestingly, at this point the Governess says that Flora loses her incredible beauty, and just seems like a regular petulant child.
- At home at Bly, Flora makes herself ill with stress, saying that she never wants to see the Governess again.
- Mrs. Grose and Flora depart for London to see the children's absent uncle.

Peter Quint Character Analysis

Peter Quint is just all kinds of trouble. On the most superficial level, he's an evil spirit who's come to haunt and/or possess little Miles. That alone would be enough to pin him as the villain of this story, but wait – there's more!

Not only is he a menacing ghostly presence, he's also a walking symbol for a whole passel of terrors. First of all, Quint stands in for the social threat of the lower classes. In life, he was an ambitious servant, who, we're led to believe, was a bit too big for his britches. Mrs. Grose tells

us that Quint didn't know his place, and that he was given too much power – once the children's uncle left Bly, Quint took control of the house and its inhabitants. Quint's character represents the breakdown of the highly structured social hierarchy that existed in James' day; while this may not seem so horrifying to us these days, it felt like a real threat back then.

Quint also represents another scary threat: sex. We know that he seduced the unfortunate Miss Jessel (their class difference also contributes to this menace; Quint is a destroyer of young ladies), and that he spent far too much time alone with young Miles. Quint is described as handsome but dastardly, and he is seductive and frightening in equal measure. Basically, Peter Quint stands for everything the Governess is afraid of, and this sense of menace is his most distinguishing characteristic.

Peter Quint Timeline and Summary

- Quint first appears to the Governess atop one of Bly's towers.
- Quint appears outside the library window.
- The Governess sees Quint actually *inside* the house for the first time – they gaze at each other and he descends the staircase and disappears.
- We don't *see* Quint, but when Miles goes out to the lawn at night, the Governess is certain that he's looking up at Quint on the tower.
- As the Governess grapples with Miles's final confession about his expulsion, Peter Quint appears one last time outside the window, his "white face of damnation" peering in – he's horrifying!

Miss Jessel Character Analysis

Interestingly enough, though she is most certainly one of the two villains of this story (from a conventional point of view, that is), we don't really know anything about Miss Jessel. We know some of her backstory – she came from a good family (she was, after all, a "lady"), and worked at Bly as the children's governess before our narrator arrived on the scene. While at Bly, she had an illicit and possibly quite racy relationship with Peter Quint; this relationship was further complicated by their class difference. However, beyond this, we really don't know anything except her physical appearance – and even that's a little sketchy. All we know is that she – or at least her ghostly form – likes to wear black, often looks weighed down by something (by misery, perhaps…or by*evil*!), and is exceptionally beautiful. Oh yeah, and she's very, very creepy…but that could just be the whole ghost thing.

Miss Jessel Timeline and Summary

- Miss Jessel appears to the Governess (and possibly Flora) by the lake.

- Prowling around the halls of the house late one night, the Governess sees Miss Jessel sitting miserably on the same staircase where she'd seen Quint earlier.
- Miss Jessel appears in the schoolroom but doesn't speak. The Governess later tells Mrs. Grose that they conversed.
- When the Governess and Mrs. Grose find Flora by the lake, the Governess sees Miss Jessel across the water again – she frantically tells the others to look at her. Mrs. Grose can't see her at all, while Flora either doesn't see her or denies that she sees her.

Mrs. Grose Character Analysis

Mrs. Grose is something of a blank page – a kindly, loving blank page, but a blank one nonetheless. We hear early on that she's been in the service of the family for a long time (she was a maid to the children's grandmother), and that she's deeply invested in the children. In general, she's really just a simple, kind, unquestioning soul; the Governess uses her both as a confidante and an informational tool, but Mrs. Grose doesn't ever act on her own. The Governess comments several times on the housekeeper's lack of imagination and her simplicity, marking her as a member of the stereotypical unintellectual working class (she's also illiterate).

Basically, Mrs. Grose is around to aid and abet the Governess, and turns out to be a loyal ally, albeit one that's not incredibly useful when it comes to action. Most of her significant scenes are simply discussions with the Governess, in which the latter lady gets information out of her, or confides what she's seen. It's also important to note that Mrs. Grose really doesn't want to believe that the children can possibly be at fault, and often questions the Governess's leaps in logic, until the very end, when she declares her allegiance to the Governess.

The Uncle Character Analysis

As you can see, the general theme here is that we don't really know anything at all about any of these characters, even our narrator. However, Miles and Flora's uncle really takes the cake for shady, mysterious characters here – we don't know his name, what he looks like, what he does, or what any of his motives are. All we know is the he's wealthy and handsome, and that these things alone win the Governess's heart from the moment she meets him.

Character Roles

Protagonist
The Governess
The Governess is certainly the protagonist of this story – she places herself in the role of heroine, even if we're ultimately not so sure what her actual role is. Since the story is told from her point of view, we only see things how she sees them; on the surface, she's a noble, heroic

savior figure (who ends up failing to save anyone), while underneath...who knows? We can see her as good through and through, or we can begin to question both her sanity and her goodness. James certainly drops a lot of clues about the moral ambiguity of the Governess, both through her similarities and odd attractions to her deceased predecessors, Quint and Jessel, and through the arrogance with which she speaks at times.

Antagonist

Peter Quint and Miss Jessel

The specter of Peter Quint is the most obvious antagonist here. He's a kind of embodiment of evil itself; the Governess's descriptions of him make it clear that he emanates some sort of malevolent force. If we are to believe everything our narrator tells us, then Quint (or Quint's ghost, to be more precise) is behind all of the things that go wrong in the story. We're meant to understand that he corrupted both Miss Jessel and Miles, and that his manipulation of Bly's inhabitants from beyond the grave is what drives the action of the story. Notably, Quint is also of a lower social standing than everyone else, except Mrs. Grose, which makes him doubly threatening – the fear here is not just of adults (or their ghosts) corrupting children, but of social inferiors corrupting the elite.

Miss Jessel is a little more complicated than her male counterpart (yes, we know, you're probably sick of seeing the word "complicated" in relation to this story by now). We're not exactly sure if she's to be feared or pitied, or both. Either way, she's certainly not a positive presence, to put it lightly.

Antagonist

Miles and Flora

This is where things grow more complicated. The way the Governess tells it, Miles and Flora are ultimately both in cahoots with the two ghosts, and are therefore antagonists – but, at the same time, she wants to save them from their evil ways. We're often alerted to the possibility that the children know about the ghosts and simply don't tell the Governess and Mrs. Grose about them; this idea of the children being corrupted by the demonic figures of Quint and Miss Jessel, both before and after their deaths, is the most horrifying thing.

However, let us not forget that we're not entirely sure about how much we can trust the Governess – just because she's our narrator for the bulk of the story doesn't mean that she's entirely honest or sane. There's always the possibility that these roles are reversed: in another reading of the story, the Governess could be seen as the antagonist, and the children as the innocent parties. We'll never know for sure what James intended us to see.

Foil

Miss Jessel (to the Governess)

Miss Jessel is interestingly aligned with the Governess; after all, she was the *previous* governess. There are many ways in which the two women seem almost to be two sides of the same coin; the dead governess had desires that she acted out with Peter Quint, while the living one has desires that she can't or won't act on (she longs for her employer). One might see Miss Jessel as the Governess gone horribly wrong. This similarity is highlighted in two scenes: first, when the Governess accidentally sinks down on the staircase in the same place where she'd seen Miss Jessel's ghost earlier, and then in the schoolroom, where both of the women

seem to have a certain right to be there – the Governess even feels like an intruder for a moment.

Companion/Informational Tool
Mrs. Grose
Good old Mrs. Grose plays the role of the levelheaded sidekick – a sort of Watson to the Governess's Sherlock Holmes. She believes the Governess instantly, and often has quite good ideas to contribute to the women's detective work. She serves many different purposes; she provides key information about Quint and Miss Jessel, and about the background of their relationships with the children, while she also eggs on the Governess, and assists her in trying to figure out what to do about the whole ghost situation.

Character Clues

Physical Appearances
Interestingly, physical appearance is the most commonly referenced mode of characterization here; people are instantly judged based on their looks, and the Governess is quick to make dramatic assumptions due to her perception of people's exteriors. For example, the children are both instantly assumed to be innocent (despite Miles's dodgy past) purely on merit of their angelic appearance, while Quint and Jessel are immediately categorized as "evil" because of their faces and figures. In fact, it's one of very few ways in which we come to understand the people that appear in this story, since we don't see the interior lives of any of the characters except the Governess.

Social Status
Social rank plays a fundamental role in telling us what to expect of characters. The world of Bly (and of Victorian England) that James depicts for us has a highly structured system of social hierarchy, and any deviation from this system instantly marks characters as bad. Quint, for example, refuses to stay within the acceptable bounds of his social position as a servant, which is what truly unnerves the characters around him. Mrs. Grose constantly comments on how Quint was "too free" (6.7) with everyone, and "did what he wished" (7.20); his transgression of the accepted boundaries between servant and master mark him as a dangerous character. On the other hand, the placid and gentle Mrs. Grose, who questions the Governess's notions but never questions her social superiority, is the image of the ideal servant, who never steps outside her bounds, and is therefore a positive character.

Literary Devices

Symbols, Imagery, Allegory

Ships, Boats
Nautical imagery occasionally appears as a symbol for – well, we're not quite sure what, but going from everything else in the story, it probably has to do with confusion and lack of

knowledge. The Governess first alludes to ships when she arrives at Bly and comments on how strange it is that she should be metaphorically steering the household, which she compares to a "great drifting ship" (1.9) full of lost passengers.

Boats make an appearance in both of the scenes at the lake with Flora, and possibly symbolize her deception of the Governess. First, the little girl attempts to build a little toy boat out of wood while the Governess, horrified, sees the ghost of Miss Jessel for the first time. In the return to the lake, Flora somehow manages to abscond with the rowboat that's usually docked at the lake and move it to a more hidden location; there's never any explanation of how or why she does this by herself, but the Governess takes it to be another sign of her dishonesty.

Unnatural Silence

Creepy, unnatural silence is a sign of Peter Quint's presence in both his first appearance and when he shows up inside the house on the staircase. In the first of these scenes, the Governess, who is strolling happily outside, notices that everything goes quiet when the mysterious figure appears, even the peaceful sounds of birdsong. This is a signal that something abnormal and certainly unnatural is happening – even though she doesn't yet know that he's a ghost yet, she can already tell that he's not meant to be there.

Inside the house, the silence is even more marked; though this close encounter seems more "human and hideous" (9.6), the lack of conversation between the Governess and her nemesis is what really makes it freaky. Finally, when the Governess actually tries to speak to one of the ghosts (Miss Jessel in the schoolroom, 15.5), the ghost does not – or cannot – answer.

"Depths" and the Unknown

OK, you've got us – this isn't exactly an image, symbol, or allegory. However, it *is* a hugely significant word, so bear with us. "Depth" is probably the most notable recurring word that shows up in the story; the Governess is always going on about how *she* has greater depths, or the *children* have depths, or how the situation as a whole has depths that are as yet unexplained. We can read this word as a stand-in for the concept of the unknown – or things that are known and hidden, which are even more dangerous.

Mrs. Grose also uses the word to describe her fear of Quint – she's afraid of him, she says, because he "was so clever – he was so deep" (6.10). We're not quite sure what lies in these depths in people, which is what makes them so scary. As you can probably tell, the Governess really loves to know things, so, naturally, things that are unknowable or undiscoverable are menacing to her, and in turn to us, as readers.

Setting

Bly, a country home in England

After the Prologue, the entire story takes place on the grounds of Bly, a remote and extensive country estate. The house is old and creepy, and from the very beginning has the air of a haunted place. We go back and forth with the Governess in finding Bly both a comforting and

disorienting space; the Governess feels more comfortable outside, where she actually gets to escape and have some alone time, but, as the story goes on, the whole estate feels more and more claustrophobic. The isolation of the characters contributes to the story's heightened sense of constant tension, since they have very little contact with the outside world, except for church on Sundays.

Narrator Point of View

First Person (principally narrated by the Governess)

We have two first person narrators throughout the course of the story. Our first narrator (who may or may not be Henry James himself, but either way, is certainly a stand-in for the figure of the author) is present only very briefly; he brings us up to speed on the origin of the story and its background info. He's notable because of his interest in the crafting of the story – through his eyes, we see the tale as a potential best seller, not necessarily as a simple story told by the fire on a winter's night.

The second narrator, who takes over in Chapter One, is of more real interest to us. She tells the story purely from her point of view – so, notably, we never really get an objective look at what's going on. Unlike some first person narrators, the Governess is totally, *totally* biased by her own thoughts and feelings, and only shows us what she's thinking and feeling…which also makes us rather suspicious of her at times.

Genre

Horror Fiction

The Turn of the Screw is one of the great horror stories of all time – since its publication, it's been incredibly influential on the genre as a whole. The most amazing thing about it is the way in which James manages to scare the pants off his readers without having to describe any gruesome or terrible things in great detail. Think about it – by leaving most of the creepy stuff up to the reader's imagination, rather than working unrelentingly to *show* us what's so scary, James succeeds in creating a haunting, memorable, and truly eerie story.

Tone

Confessional, Direct, Biased

James cultivates a tone of honest, direct discourse in the Governess's manuscript; in so doing, he works to preserve the fictional frame of the story – remember, we're supposed to believe that this is a real-life manuscript that relates a real-life story. The tone he affects to make this scenario seem possible is extremely straightforward, with a kind of "tell-all" quality to it; we're obviously seeing the events through the highly biased eyes of the Governess. This

accomplishes two very important things: first of all, James successfully creates a narrator who is lifelike and emotional; secondly, he constructs a narrator who is untrustworthy and questionable precisely *because* she is so lifelike.

Writing Style

Highly Structured, Carefully Constructed, Writerly

This story is a fascinating example of the difference between tone and style. While James adopts a highly emotional, somewhat melodramatic, and intensely personal tone in writing the Governess's narrative, he maintains a style that is tightly reined-in and highly structured. We get the feeling simultaneously that the narrator (the Governess) is gradually losing control, while the author (James) consistently works to create the *illusion* of lost control.

James's amazing use of pacing and his masterful creation of suspense is evident most clearly at the end of the story. The chapters grow shorter and shorter, building to the final moment (Chapter Twenty-Four), in which Quint appears for the last time, and Miles unexpectedly expires – and then it just stops.

Upon a first read, the average reader is like, "*What*? That's not what I was waiting for! Thanks a lot, Henry *Lame*!" However, the more you ponder this ending, the more absolutely perfect it is – by not revealing anything at all, James allows his readers to keep mulling it over in their minds. Though at first it seems to be an incredibly flawed conclusion, perhaps more in keeping with the lack of control demonstrated in the Governess's voice, we ultimately see that James knew exactly what he was doing here, and that the whole story is constructed to culminate in this moment of shock and frustration.

What's Up With the Title?

This title's meaning is exposed on the very first page of the story; after hearing a ghoulish tale in which a child is menaced by some ghostly terror, someone suggests that the fact that the story's protagonist was a child is what gives a certain "turn of the screw" – that is, it tightens the dramatic tension. James' story offers a *second* "turn" by introducing a horror story about *two* children instead of one. This is an oddly mechanical way of describing the construction of a horror story – that is, a story that cranks the audience's stress level way up – and it keeps one of James's primary concerns, the craft of writing, in the back of the reader's mind at all times. The title also takes on a second meaning as we near the end of the story; the protagonist uses the phrase to describe taking control of her mental and emotional capabilities in preparation for a challenge.

What's Up With the Ending?

Hmm, good question – what *is* up with this ending? Basically, the story leaves us right in the middle of things. If you're stumped by the rapid-fire sequence of events of the last chapter, don't worry – so are we, and so is everyone. Does the ghost of Peter Quint finally overwhelm

Miles and kill him? Does the boy's shock and terror squeeze the life out of him? Does the Governess herself murder him? What? Huh? Why?!

James, being the rascal that he is, obviously intends for his readers to reach the end and be totally confused. The ambiguity of events and of the cause of Miles's death is clearly the key to understanding the actual *truth* of the story – however, rather than give all of this away to us, James just *stops* at the point of revealing everything.

This isn't just laziness, folks, it's genius. Think about it – by refusing to tell his readers what really happens to Miles (and therefore refusing to tell us if the Governess is trustworthy or not), he leaves an indelible imprint on the reader's mind. Instead of sitting back and being told a story, we are forced to engage with it, and to attempt to figure it out ourselves. While it may be grossly unsatisfying the first time you read it, trust us – the more you mull it over, the more fascinating (and *awesome*!) this ambiguous, infuriating ending becomes.

Did You Know?

Trivia

- *The Turn of the Screw* was actually adapted into a popular opera by superstar English composer Benjamin Britten in 1954. (Source)
- Interestingly, the story may have been inspired by an actual (possibly "true" story) told to James by his friend, E.W. Benson, the Archbishop of Canterbury. (Source: Curtis, Anthony. Introduction. *The Turn of the Screw and the Aspern Papers*. By Henry James. London: Penguin, 1984)

Steaminess Rating

PG

OK, so there's no sex overtly mentioned in this story –it is, after all, a Victorian story about children. But *The Turn of the Screw* gets a "P" added to that "G" simply because of the implied ick factor. There are a lot of secretly icky, weird feelings in the mix here...between Quint and Miss Jessel, Quint and Miles, the Governess and the children's uncle, and, most of all, between Miles and the Governess. Sure, nobody even mentions sex – the topic was forbidden in polite fiction at the time – but we have to wonder what the characters are *really* thinking about each other.

Allusions and Cultural References

Literature and Philosophy

- Ann Radcliffe, *The Mysteries of Udolpho* (4.1)
- Henry Fielding, *Amelia* (9.4)
- David and Saul, Biblical figures (18.3)

Pop Culture

- Mrs. Jane Marcet (10.5)

Best of the Web

Movie or TV Productions

The Turn of the Screw, 1999
http://www.imdb.com/title/tt0209440/
A recent-ish BBC version, starring Colin Firth.

In a Dark Place, 2006
http://www.imdb.com/title/tt0460435/
A recent modern interpretation…

Britten's *Turn of the Screw*, 2004
http://www.imdb.com/title/tt0469044/
Here's the most recent filmed version of the Britten opera, adapted from the story.

Videos

Colin "Mr. Darcy" Firth in *The Turn of the Screw*
http://www.youtube.com/watch?v=Oe2Nv3n8Mv4
Here's the beginning to the 1999 BBC version of the story.

Now, with music!
http://www.youtube.com/watch?v=SVdUIL9JYXM
A snippet of the famed Benjamin Britten opera.

The Others trailer
http://www.youtube.com/watch?v=Vu494-Dr5po

While not totally derived from *The Turn of the Screw*, *The Others* seems to have been influenced by James's story.

Images

The Turn of the Screw on Lost!
http://www.losthatch.com/images%5Cscreen_captures%5CS2E03_The_Turn_Of_The_Screw.jpg
The book made a brief guest appearance on the popular TV series.

This one gives us the shivers...
http://www.jssgallery.org/Paintings/Portrait_of_Edouard_and_Marie-Loise_Pailleron.jpg
Here's the creepy John Singer Sargent painting that's on our cover of   *Turn of the Screw* (the Penguin Classics edition).

Websites

Turn of the Screw e-text
http://www.gutenberg.org/etext/209
Here's an online version from the ever-useful Project Gutenberg site.

The Henry James Scholar's Guide to Websites
http://www2.newpaltz.edu/~hathaway/
Well, a guide to James-related sites, at least.

The Ladder
http://www.henryjames.org.uk/
A great place to start for online research on Henry James.